'*GIS for Planning and the Built Environment* is a rea
and refreshing approach to GIS. This text provides a
of GIS and spatial analysis concepts and refers to
should be useful to planners. The book has a unive
range of GIS principles that can be implemented acr⌐⌐
– **Les Dolega**, *University of Liverpool, UK*

'*GIS for Planning and the Built Environment* is a brilliant take on the current state
of Geographic Information Systems across the globe and is a must-read for planners,
students and GIS technicians. Ferrari and Rae's ability to expertly capture and describe
the history and future of Geographic Information Systems seems effortless. A quick and
engaging read, this book would make an excellent textbook for college-level GIS and/or
Planning classes. I highly recommend it!'
– **Tony Giarrusso**, *Georgia Institute of Technology, USA*

'This book walks the reader through the thought processes that are needed to go from
having a bit of geographical data to analysing and presenting it in a clear and effective
way. The strength of this book is that provides a toolkit of approaches and applications
which are independent of technology, software and location. It is also written in a user
friendly style that will make it a useful text for many students, practitioners and professionals in the fields of GIS, planning and the built environment.'
– **Ruth Hamilton**, *University of Sheffield, UK*

'*GIS for Planning and the Built Environment* provides a "why to guide" to the potential
of GIS, accompanied by contemporary examples and applications. It is the perfect text
for students accessing GIS for the first time as it showcases the potential and recent
explosion of demand for geo-visualisation, communication and accessibility of spatial
data.'
– **Damien Mansell**, *University of Exeter, UK*

'This book expertly weaves together the applied and the academic, the conceptual and
the technical. It explains in a very clear manner a range of spatial analytical techniques
that can be applied to evidence-based planning in an increasingly complex and nuanced
world. It will serve as an excellent text in upper-level undergraduate or graduate-level
courses.'
– **Siqing Chen**, *University of Melbourne, Australia*

'This book represents a good first step towards learning the use of GIS methods for
planners. I find it useful both for students and for professionals within the field, with its
focus on applied methods and with many relevant practical examples. I'm particularly
pleased that network analysis has been included here, a topic applicable for planning
that I have missed in many of the generic GIS textbooks available elsewhere.'
– **Yngve Karl Frøyen**, *Norwegian University of Science
and Technology, Norway*

'GIS and planning have both undergone substantial change in recent decades –
the authors are ideally placed to traverse these developments and to provide a much
needed update on the relationship between the two fields. They tackle the hype sur-
rounding GIS in order to demonstrate its relevance to contemporary urban planning
processes and problems. All too often GIS lecturers may be unfamiliar with the best
means to approach these issues with planning students, while their planning colleagues
may struggle to keep abreast of GIS. This book successfully fills this gap in an engaging
and accessible style and with a range of well-chosen examples.'
– **Alistair Geddes**, *University of Dundee, UK*

planning • environment • cities

Series Editors: Yvonne Rydin and Ben Clifford*

The context in which planning operates has changed dramatically in recent years. Economic processes have become increasingly globalised and economic fortunes have fluctuated. Not only have administrations in various countries changed, but old ideologies have been swept away and new ones have tentatively emerged. A new environmental agenda has prioritised the goal of sustainable development, requiring continued action at international, national and local levels.

Cities are today faced with new pressures for economic competiveness, greater accountability and participation, improved quality of life for citizens, and global environmental responsibilities. These pressures are often contradictory and create difficult dilemmas for policy-makers, especially in the context of fiscal austerity.

In these changing circumstances, planners, from many backgrounds, in many different organisations, have come to re-evaluate their work. They have to engage with actors in government, the private sector and non-governmental organisations in discussions over the role of planning in relation to the environment and cities. The intention of the *Planning, Environment, Cities* series is to explore the changing nature of planning and contribute to the debate about its future.

This series is primarily aimed at students and practitioners of planning and such related professions as estate management, housing and architecture as well as those in politics, public and social administration, geography and urban studies. It comprises both general texts and books designed to make a more particular contribution, in both cases characterised by: an international approach; extensive use of case studies; and emphasis on contemporary relevance and the application of theory to advance planning practice.

* Andrew Thornley was series co-editor with Yvonne Rydin up to his retirement from the role in January 2017.

planning • environment • cities

Series Editors: Yvonne Rydin and Ben Clifford

Published

Philip Allmendinger
  Planning Theory (3rd edn)
Luca Bertolini
  Planning the Mobile Metropolis
Jon Coaffee and Peter Lee
  Urban Resilience: Planning for Risk, Crisis and Uncertainty
Chris Couch
  Urban Planning: An Introduction
Ed Ferrari and Alasdair Rae
  GIS for Planning and the Built Environment: An Introduction to Spatial Analysis
Ruth Fincher and Kurt Iveson
  Planning and Diversity in the City: Redistribution, Recognition and Encounter
Cliff Hague, Euan Hague and Carrie Breitbach
  Regional and Local Economic Development
Patsy Healey
  Collaborative Planning (2nd edn)
Patsy Healey
  Making Better Places: The Planning Project in the 21st Century
Simon Joss
  Sustainable Cities: Governing for Urban Innovation
Ted Kitchen
  Skills for Planning Practice
Ali Madanipour
  Urban Design, Space and Society
Peter Newman and Andrew Thornley
  Planning World Cities (2nd edn)
Michael Oxley
  Economics, Planning and Housing
Dory Reeves
  Management Skills for Effective Planners
Yvonne Rydin
  Urban and Environmental Planning in the UK (2nd edn)
Mark Tewdwr-Jones
  Spatial Planning and Governance: Understanding UK Planning
Geoff Vigar, Patsy Healey, Angela Hull and Simin Davoudi
  Planning, Governance and Spatial Strategy in Britain: An Institutionalist Analysis
Iain White
  Environmental Planning in Context

Other titles planned include
International Planning Studies
Contemporary Planning Practice

GIS for Planning and the Built Environment

An Introduction to Spatial Analysis

Ed Ferrari and Alasdair Rae

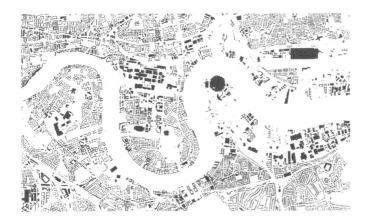

First published 2019 by
RED GLOBE PRESS

Red Globe Press in the UK is an imprint of Springer Nature Limited, registered in England, company number 785998, of 4 Crinan Street, London, N1 9XW.

Red Globe Press® is a registered trademark in the United States, the United Kingdom, Europe and other countries.

ISBN 978–1–137–30715–6 hardback
ISBN 978–1–137–30714–9 paperback

A catalogue record for this book is available from the British Library.

A catalog record for this book is available from the Library of Congress.

Contents

List of Figures, Tables and Boxes

Figures

Tables

Boxes

Acknowledgements

The authors would like to acknowledge in particular the inspiration of the late Waldo Tobler, pictured below with the authors in 2013. We are very grateful to Waldo's wife, Rachel Tobler, for giving us permission to use this photo. We are also very grateful to our families for bearing with us over the years as this book project has come to fruition. We also thank the many hundreds of students at the University of Sheffield whom we have been fortunate to teach over the years, and colleagues who have helped us think more deeply about GIS and spatial analysis. We would also like to thank the following people for support, inspiration, assistance or guidance at various times during the life of this project: Stephen Wenham, who originally commissioned the text; Andrew Malvern, who has seen it through to the finish line; Lauren Ferreira, whose attention to detail ensured that the images are legible and used legally; Addy Pope, who has always been a friend of GIS in Higher Education; and Ruth Hamilton for helpful suggestions and comments. We also thank the anonymous reviewers of the manuscript for helping us sharpen our ideas.

The authors, with the late Waldo Tobler in Santa Barbara, 2013

Chapter 1

Introduction

Introduction

Despite being a recognised part of the planner's toolbox for more than three decades, geographic information systems (GIS) can still possess a kind of mystique: excitement about their capabilities, mixed with the sort of fear and admiration of the skilled user that might be found as one regards a neurosurgeon. This mystique is not deserved. It should not be this way.

Although the sometimes overblown claims of tech professionals and software companies might lead us to think otherwise, GIS users – unlike, say, neurosurgeons – do not actually save lives in their day-to-day work. Yet, as has been known for some time, cartographers wield a sort of power that has very often been used for ill rather than good, and the safest and fairest conclusion might be, in the words of Mark Monmonier, that maps lie.

But a good part of the reason why GIS commands hushed admiration and respect is because of its potential to transform the communication of complex ideas about society, about cities and the impacts of policies, about the unevenness that pervades every aspect of life on Earth. GIS was at the forefront of the 'big data' revolution, for example, given that the vast majority – and an increasing amount – of information is also information specifically about places somewhere on the planet. From football clubs to Twitter conversations, government spending to the spread of diseases, these can be mapped, and not just as part of a trivial, academic exercise in analytical one-upmanship, but because by mapping it we can genuinely see patterns, tell stories and infer things in a way that we sometimes cannot by poring over tables and spreadsheets and charts. That is the heart of what might be called spatial analysis, and it is these possibilities that are uniquely unlocked by a computational approach to dealing with geographical information.

Map-making is an inescapable part of planning practice, even if it is no longer its central activity. Planning is fundamentally about land; and yet it is also about contestation and the mediation of opposing viewpoints and sets of values. A good planner sees not only the map but also the process and has the skills of diplomacy and dialogue to understand not only 'how to get there' but also where it is that we want, or need, to get to. In that sense, planning is a communicative art, with information – both tacit and technical – flowing both from planner to stakeholders and vice versa. Maps are a great communication tool, but they are not the only tool, just as technical evidence is not the only raw material the planner must deal with.

1

This is a book about using GIS in the planning of the built environment. It is first and foremost a practical volume: it is designed to inspire but also to lead readers through the possibilities of using GIS and spatial analysis within the broad realm of spatial planning practice. But it is not a technical guide, even if we do provide some useful practical guidance in Chapter 6. It is not the intention to provide a narrow, technocentric view of the world. Rather, it starts from the premise that planners are dealing with so-called 'wicked problems', in the environment, in society, in the economy. Planners are part of the solution, but they are not the solution alone; they need to talk with others, use others' information and – most critically – implement processes of consultation and plan-making that involve communities and lead to better places and better outcomes for people.

Working with data and information about places is central to this, and that is where GIS comes in. The central purpose of the book is to allow those with an interest in planning the built environment – be they professional planners themselves, residents, students, civil servants, elected community representatives, businesses or academics – some way of understanding the art of the possible with regards to the application of GIS and spatial analysis to the problems they face, and putting it into practice. The democratisation of data and – with the advent of open source software – the technologies themselves, means that for the first time in that 40-plus-year history, GIS can truly be a tool for everyone and not just for those with power.

Who is this book aimed at?

All the above leads to the question, who should be reading this book? In short, anyone with an interest in applying GIS methods to planning problems. It will also be useful to anyone using GIS in a built environment context more generally. The book assumes a basic understanding of information technology but does not require specialist knowledge of data analysis, GIS or spatial analysis. More important is the imagination to understand spatial problems and the way that analysis of information could help yield insights into them. This means that planners and students of planning are not the only groups that will find this book useful. Indeed, the city councillor wishing to write a neighbourhood plan and who wants to know how to get information on housing and map it, or the business wanting to understand how to improve its analysis of its local customer base, will find much within this book to interest them.

We now live in the very privileged position that, in Europe and North America as indeed throughout much of the world, the move is inexorably towards the opening up of access to data. This includes the vastly expensive digital mapping resources that taxpayers have traditionally funded but have until recently had no way of freely accessing. A good example of this is in Great Britain, where Ordnance Survey (the national mapping agency) have made vast archives of spatial data available. Spurred on in part by technological advances in data management and delivery, but also by shifts in expectations around governance and transparency, the default position regarding access to these vast data resources is increasingly to make them openly accessible, albeit with some restrictions.

At the same time, private global corporations have funded incredible new geospatial data resources, whether it be Google Maps, Bing Maps, satellite imagery and addressing resources, or the geotagging of just about every object on the Internet. Even geospatial data from several Space Shuttle missions is now freely available on the Internet courtesy of NASA. Incredibly useful as these resources are, they are not *always* open, and some remain proprietary and 'read only'. Thus, even more exciting is the maturity of the open source, distributed and 'crowdfunded' approach to major data generation challenges, such as that of mapping the world as the fantastic OpenStreetMap project has done.

This open approach now extends into the production of the very tools and techniques we can use. The free availability for several years of useful but somewhat cumbersome and specialist toolkits like GRASS has now yielded fruit in projects like QGIS, which bring together open source toolkits and user-written modules and present them in a user-friendly and freely available cross-platform environment. It is only the beginning when we see several city governments across the globe building their corporate GIS capabilities around QGIS, in so doing doubtless causing sleepless nights for account managers throughout the GIS software industry.

The consequence of this new world is that we are at a point where the readership for a book like this ought not to be confined to professional planners and students but to those from all walks of life who want to, or need to, engage with the full apparatus of place-making machinery, agonistically or peaceably, and who need evidence to make their case. We do not aim to provide a comprehensive account of the world of GIS; that is too big a task, and is not the aim here anyway. Instead, we focus on what we believe is most important for students of planning and the built environment, though we do not assume a high level of prior knowledge.

That said, a working knowledge of how planning systems work or what planning is (in any national context) will help the reader. By this, we mean the ways in which the production and reproduction of the built environment are achieved, the key social, economic and environmental resources that go into this endeavour, and the ways that it is regulated and governed. The specifics and the principles vary from place to place, of course, but throughout the world such systems are united by their focus on spatial relations, or the spatial contexts for and implications of other key societal relations, such as power relations. This is not intended to be a theory-heavy text, but we do start from the point of view – mentioned above – that planning is a process with communication at its heart. Consequently, we are keen to emphasise in this book the communicative power of GIS, alongside its analytical capabilities, and this is covered in more depth in Chapter 5, on geovisualisation.

Aims and objectives

Hopefully, the reader who has got this far sees themselves in one of the roles pictured above. They understand the problems, and are thirsty for ways of designing the analytical tools that help them get further insight. This book aims to equip those readers with the knowledge, skills and experience to understand how spatial analysis can help them to understand spatial planning problems. The focus throughout will be on commonly available tools. The book aims to fill the gap between very theoretical, abstract treatments of GIS (e.g. from the organisational or information management perspective) and those that are heavy with the arcane methodological and technical material that characterises some of the more specialised texts. This book is no more a 'how-to' guide as it is a 'why' guide: why would we use GIS in a particular given circumstance; to understand a particular given problem? Then how might we do it?

The book arose from a recognition that there were very few – if any – contemporary texts that really took as their starting point the kind of socioeconomic problems that planners face. Many of the textbooks are multidisciplinary in nature, but this means that some of the techniques are described in a way that is very difficult to translate them to the language of the built environment. In our work, we routinely use spatial analysis techniques and software tools that were designed by physical geographers wishing to model environmental processes to, instead, get some insight into social phenomena. Seen at the scale of the city, for example, house prices have 'gradients' and 'surfaces', just as sand dunes do, and it is sometime helpful to think of social and economic issues using different lenses when trying to understand the bigger picture.

So this book is a little bit translational in nature: hopefully, the reader will find that techniques that were developed with some other purpose in mind translate with a little imagination to the problems inherent in the built environment and its planning.

It is hoped that readers of this book will:

- Obtain the knowledge, skill and experience to understand how the spatial analysis of data about the 'real world' can be used to understand planning problems;
- Be able to apply a broad range of spatial analytic and visualisation techniques using industry standard GIS software packages; and
- Understand how maps and data can be used effectively as evidence for planning-related issues.

Structure of the book

In pursuit of the above aims and objectives, the book adopts a structure that begins by looking at why GIS is particularly useful for planning and the built environment. It then moves on to consider in more detail what is special about GIS, in the sense that it is a spatial database of our world. Owing to its centrality to GIS, we then look at data as 'the currency of GIS' before going on to look at the communicative power of it though geovisualisation. This is followed by a more practical chapter on mapping the built environment before we take two key analytical approaches – spatial analysis and network analysis – and provide more detail and examples of why they are so important. The final chapter attempts to bring all this together and reflects on key messages.

There are several important points of departure from the wisdoms or perspectives that might be propounded by other GIS texts, and it would be advisable for the reader to at least familiarise themselves with these. Rather than develop a thematic structure that is driven by data or methods, we adopt three key themes that are related to what we see as the principal advantages of using GIS. These themes, which are woven into the fabric of the text throughout the book, are:

- *Improved understanding* of spatial phenomena;
- *Efficient management* of planning processes; and
- *Enhanced communication* of ideas between stakeholders.

Chapter 2 sets the scene by tackling the question, 'why GIS for planning and the built environment?'. We seek to move beyond the rather simple idea that planners use GIS because planners use maps. Rather, we want to get to the idea that planners need to use GIS because it helps answer questions and it helps communicate ideas. In this chapter, we begin by reflecting on GIS's origins as a technical, scientific subject and its relationship with planning, where it has often been seen as a tool of the 'specialist' rather than the generalist. We challenge this view here and argue that the world – and GIS – has moved on and it is time for planning to re-assess GIS and re-engage with it. Yes, planning is a complex discipline but it also needs good mapping and spatial analysis and we can learn much from looking at GIS afresh and put maps firmly back in planning. We look at GIS from four different perspectives here: as a tool for description, as a discipline in itself (as in geographical information science or GIScience), as a tool for engagement and public communication, and as a way of learning in relation to GIS for education. We also urge caution in relation to the use of GIS, by referring to Maslow's so-called 'law of the instrument': 'I suppose it is tempting, if the only tool you have is a hammer, to treat everything as if it were a nail.' Ultimately, we argue for the importance of GIS in planning and the built environment and suggest that it is too important to be left to the specialists.

Chapters 3 and 4 put in place the essential concepts that we think are important to comprehend when using GIS to tackle planning issues. The first is the idea that, actually, GIS is not really about map-making at all: it is about an explicitly spatial approach to managing *data*. We contend in Chapter 3 that GIS is best understood not from the starting point of the map (and seeking to explain its development as the digital equivalent of cartography) but from the starting point of the data (seeing its development as a digital spatial database). GIS is a spatial database of our world. It does all the things that 'traditional' databases do: organise collections of data so that questions can be efficiently posed of those collections of data, while bringing to the database paradigm the killer weapon: *geography*. Being able to answer questions related to geography, such as '*where* do things happen?' or 'what is *near* me?', extends the scope of the idea of a database hugely. But, of course, databases and the computing platforms on which they sit have their own special languages. GIS is built on those, too. This is why GIS can too often seem like a computing technology, aimed squarely at a closed group of techies, than something of use for multidisciplinary generalists like planners, designers, politicians or activists. This chapter introduces some of the basic database concepts and terminologies and attempts to show how these apply within GIS software by using some real-world metaphors. The chapter also discusses how the efficacy of any spatial model of the world built up from data relies on some fundamental concepts such as accuracy, precision, scale and generalisation.

Having proposed the fundamental idea of GIS as a spatial database as more useful to planners than the idea of GIS as cartography, we next look at the raw material itself: data. **Chapter 4** discusses data as the 'currency of GIS' and seeks to understand its true value within the context of the need for planners to move beyond superficial ideas about 'knowledge' towards a more informationally rich understanding of 'wisdom'. In other words, data helps us answer questions. But handled well it also helps us to identify new questions. In an era of 'big data' and massive, freely available spatial datasets, it is more urgent than ever to have a clear, systematic approach towards identifying and answering questions and the role of data in that. We are not interested in, nor would we support, the idea of just throwing data at a problem to see what sticks. Chapter 4 also provides a wealth of practical tips on how to use datasets within GIS, and how to understand the myriad different file formats that are used to store mapping data, tabular data and the other raw data resources used within GIS.

Chapter 5 extends the idea of the map into the realm of *geovisualisation*, which places a particular emphasis on the communicative power of maps and spatial data and the role of these in planning discourse. This chapter explains why 'geovisualisation' is not just a fancy term for 'mapping' but a considered art and science of 'condensing and abstracting and indexing the great buzzing confusion of information that comes from the world around us' (Boulding, 1970, p. 2). The increasing sophistication of the role of visual language in maps is demonstrated by reference to 3D mapping, interactive maps, animation and maps which play around with space itself (for example, maps emphasising connectivity or time over distance). The chapter discusses the problems that arise from having *too much* data, and presents practical ways of synthesising, analysing and presenting spatial information, at all times mindful of a set of principles of the 'orderly loss of information'. A range of good practice examples and case studies are provided.

In **Chapter 6**, we attempt to provide a more practical guide to mapping and the built environment. We do this because we want to provide readers with a resource they can return to again and again for advice about making maps with GIS. Part art and part science, the activity of making maps is fraught with complexity, and without careful thought it is very easy to produce misleading maps. In fact, the ease with which we can produce maps in modern GIS packages now sometimes seems inversely proportional to the quality of maps we see in the public domain. *That is, it is now very easy to make maps but it remains very difficult to make good maps.* We offer advice here that we hope will help improve maps from both a technical and a communicative perspective. This is not an exhaustive coverage but we do look at some of the most common map types, including land use maps, choropleth maps and mapping the urban fabric, in addition to individual map elements like titles, scale bars and legends.

The final pair of chapters before the conclusion (Chapter 9) deal more explicitly with *spatial analysis* – formal techniques by which the spatial arrangement of entities and phenomena in the real world can be studied with a view to generating new knowledge and insight. **Chapter 7** takes as its starting point the late Waldo Tobler's famous 'First Law of Geography': that 'everything is related to everything else, but near things are more related than distant things' (Tobler, 1970, p. 236). This is used to set out the key principles for the use of spatial analysis in answering a set of specifically *spatial* questions in relation to planning and the built environment. The role of integrated processes of analysis, involving different tools in helping to provide insights, is discussed. The chapter cautions, however, against the view of GIS and spatial analysis as a hegemonic approach that serves to exclude other forms of knowledge. As we say in the introduction to Chapter 7, the optimal approach to a planning problem will require 'a careful mix of spatial analytical and people-centred decision making'.

Chapter 8 is about connectivity. It shows how the use of 'network analysis' can be used to solve tricky planning problems where distance is not the prime concern but where time, costs or other measures of connectedness might be more important. This chapter shows how many core GIS concepts explicitly or implicitly favour Euclidean geometry and the role of straight-line distance, but that in some important cases planners need a more nuanced understanding of space. The chapter defines key terminology used in network models and shows how such models have actually come to pervade many aspects of modern life, being as they are the backbone to such technologies as satellite navigation and critical in achieving optimality in the delivery of parcels or fast food, or the routing of public transport or Uber cabs. The key classes of 'network problem' are set out in this chapter, together with strategies for solving them using GIS tools.

Finally, **Chapter 9** turns its attention to the key problem that is associated with everything else the book covers: *how can better decisions be made?* In this chapter we return to the types of issues and problems typically facing planners, and we discuss how the information and wisdom that might come from the application of GIS and spatial analysis might be deployed within a broader framework of decision making. We consider some common pitfalls in presenting maps and the products of spatial analysis within broader decision-making structures such as those found within government and private companies, and how best to account for uncertainty within GIS models. We look at the example of multi-criteria evaluation methods as a way of bringing together information on a range of different factors to help guide decision making. We also sound a cautionary note around the heavy premium that is placed on 'ground-truthing' data, 'road-testing' analytical approaches and building and maintaining stake-holder consensus.

How to use this book

It may seem odd to include advice on 'how to use' a book, yet it is important because we did not write this book as one that can or should be read sequentially in one sitting. It is designed to support a programme of learning, perhaps across an academic semester or perhaps over the course of a year as readers are learning GIS. If you want to learn how to use a particular GIS package that is normally best done through taught sessions with a professor or at a professional training event, or in directed learning courses online. If you want comprehensive coverage of GIS from beginning to end, then we recommend readers refer to Longley and colleagues' (2015) *Geographic Information Systems and Science*, now in its fourth edition and firmly established as a classic and comprehensive overview text.

If you are a student of city, urban, regional planning or just interested in the subject and how GIS can help you, what it can do, and how to make better maps and conduct sound analysis then this textbook is aimed at you. With this in mind, each individual chapter can be read as a stand-alone piece and Chapter 6 in particular is intended to provide the kind of practical guidance that can help you make better maps, or just more accurately assess the quality and validity of existing ones.

With this in mind, we end this chapter by posing a number of questions and suggesting which part of the book you might turn to if you want to find an answer. At times, with some important topics, we use text in separate boxes if a particular issue is of great importance so that they are easier to find.

How can I make better maps?

For this, turn to **Chapter 6**. We include specific advice on different map types, but also on the use of colour, data classification and mapping at different scales, and we also suggest three principles of a 'good map': simplicity, appropriateness and value added.

What do I need to know about data in GIS?

In this book, we refer to data as being the 'currency' of GIS because of its importance and the inability to do much without it. We provide examples of the kinds of data you may come across and explain the relationship between data, information, knowledge and wisdom. We also discuss how this is not necessarily a simple relationship! For this, see **Chapter 4**.

I'm looking for inspiration: what new stuff can you show me?

In order to highlight the fact that GIS is about so much more than making simple static maps, **Chapter 5** has been put together partly to educate readers on what is possible and partly to inspire readers about what is possible.

Why does everyone go on about the 'First Law of Geography'?

If you take a class in GIS or spatial analysis, or any kind of quantitative geography, you are likely to come across Waldo Tobler's famous – and often misunderstood – 'First Law of Geography'. Here we attempt to explain it more simply in relation to spatial analysis, in **Chapter 7**. We also refer to the lesser-known 'Second Law of Geography', which we think is important, and often overlooked.

Chapter 2

Why GIS and Planning for the Built Environment?

Introduction

In the context of contemporary theory about planning and the built environment, GIS may appear to be something of a throwback. It harks back to a past era in which planning was characterised as a technical, scientific process in which optimal solutions to clearly agreed problems could be sought. This inevitably led to the promotion of the 'expert', enabled by a benign social and cultural environment where science and technology – including, arguably, the technologies of government itself – enjoyed levels of public trust and respect that would today be unthinkable. The grand challenges of the day were framed in positivism, in which the focus was on scientific verification and quantitative data, giving rise to physical responses to problems that were described and financed in gigantic terms. The challenges of post-war reconstruction, of winning a nuclear arms race, and providing the infrastructure demanded by new forms of global economic interactions, as well as the understanding of societal and economic challenges concomitant to these pursuits, all lent themselves to the type of rational problem solving and engineering responses that characterised a modernist watershed in spatial planning.

Planning was then more a science than an art, arguably aided by a political consensus around the necessity of planning on the type of scale, and accepting the commensurate risks, demanded by the huge motorway, housing and energy projects of the day. Disciplines such as sociology, geography and politics began to absorb the language of the economist and statistician, bringing to bear on their respective fields a quest for numerical precision and quantification. The quantitative revolution in geography unleashed a momentous paradigmatic shift in the way the subject was understood: a more systematic, more analytic and abstract understanding of space began to replace the exploratory and anthropological. It was perhaps no less colonial in its underlying philosophy, but the new geographers and planners sought to conquer new worlds not through the discovery, exchange and appropriation of cultural artefacts but through the ordering and categorising of space; subjecting unfamiliar terrains to the dispassionate calculus of optimality. If the means were different, the end remained the pursuit of economic progress and growth. As Richard Klosterman put it, underlying 'traditional' arguments for planning was the belief that the conscious application of professional expertise, instrumental rationality, and scientific methods could more effectively promote economic growth and political stability than the unplanned forces of market and political competition.

(Klosterman, 1985, p. 13)

That traditional world is not the world of planning that this book speaks to, even if it is the type of planning that gave rise to the analytical techniques and computational capabilities that form the foundation of modern GIS. Planning now is much more distinctly an art: an art that is less plastic and more political in nature, and demands in planners a level of delicacy in judgement, evaluation and synthesis that was not necessarily the most important part of the traditional job description that valued objective calculation. This has come at a cost, and it is doubtless the case that today's planners lack the confidence and fluency in quantitative techniques that their predecessors took for granted as part of their toolkit. Without denigrating the achievements of those involved in 'planning' (in the broadest sense) our current built environment it is undoubtedly the case that the job of planning today is more complex than before in several important respects.

First, planners need to reconcile not only competing land uses but also competing ideologies and values that underpin the perspectives of different stakeholders. Many have talked about the 'triple bottom line' of securing simultaneously the maximal economic, social and environmental outcomes for any given locality; critics like Campbell (1996) point out that this is an impossible and theoretically incoherent task. Consequently, planners need to take sides and may need to be driven by a normative vision. But whose?

Second, planners must respond to complex government initiatives that are often contradictory, short-termist, or may misdiagnose the 'problem'. Take the simple case of education policy in most developed economies. Although it is a gross simplification, it is nevertheless true to say that while on the one hand land use planners have striven to reduce the need to travel through more intelligent zoning, education planners have at the same time promoted choices that actively involve sending children to distant schools (Ferrari and Green, 2013).

Third, the state as an all-seeing, all-doing entity has retreated significantly. This reflects a different philosophy about how places should be governed but also the idea that the public sector cannot, and must not, deliver everything in the built environment, such as housing. Associated with this has been recent severe funding cuts to local governments across the world. A report by the *Financial Times* in the United Kingdom, for example, estimates that between 2015 and 2020 local councils in England will have experienced a 77% cut in core funding.

Finally, and perhaps most importantly, the planning profession no longer benefits from the kind of optimism that we saw in much of Europe and North America in the years after 1945 until the mid-1970s. Planning enjoyed much public support and was a highly visible enterprise, with major new infrastructure projects, mass housebuilding, new towns and the total redevelopment of many urban areas all contributing to the sense that planning was in the ascendancy. This is no longer the case, but in this we see an opportunity. With careful, thoughtful engagement with GIS and spatial analysis techniques, and particularly by using GIS as a communicative tool rather than as a representation of how our world 'should be', it can help reinvigorate planning and other built environment disciplines.

Given these factors, and the need to help situate GIS and spatial analysis within a wider context for planning and the built environment, this chapter provides further context about what GIS is, what it does and how it can help us.

GIS and planning

The first thing we need to think about here is the basic relationship between GIS and planning. We think of planning in the formal sense of it as a distinct discipline, with trained professionals working in government or private practice. But we are also thinking in relation to planning education (e.g. at universities or in professional education) and engagement with the wider public. As we have said above, GIS emerged during a more scientific, technocratic era and, today, planning is characterised less by the idea of problems and solutions but by complexity and nuance.

For some people, this does not necessarily sit easily with GIS and spatial analysis and this is the point at which critics would normally claim there is no significant role for GIS in planning today, but we would strongly disagree. Central to the discipline of planning, however we understand it, has been spatial representations of places, and planning is fundamentally about space: how it is used, who owns it, what can be done with it, how it is managed and so on. Most often, the spatial representations seen in planning are maps that show, for example, how a neighbourhood is zoned, where a new railway line might be built or the proposed location of new housing. We may also see 3D interactive models of cities, small-scale models of cities and even virtual reality depictions of cities that we can walk around. Such activities are not specific to any one country, and so this means that GIS ought to have global appeal and can help planners in any national context. That is partly why we have used examples from different countries in this book; to demonstrate that, although we are based in the United Kingdom, GIS is international in its utility and appeal.

Yet if we look at many planning textbooks today there are often no maps or spatial representations at all, and it seems that in many ways the links between geography and planning have been weakened. On the one hand, this is a reflection of a key truth in that planning is also about people, politics and ideology and should and will therefore always be about more than maps and plans. But without these we would argue that planning really is missing a key ingredient and one that can play a key role in the rehabilitation of planning in the public eye. That is part of our aim with this book, but in this chapter we will reflect briefly on the following four ideas in order to set the scene: (1) GIS as a tool for description; (2) GIS as a discipline in itself, and one that can help answer and find questions; (3) GIS for engagement and public communication; and (4) GIS for education, in universities and elsewhere.

GIS for describing our world

When we talk about 'GIS' we need to be clear about what we mean. Throughout this book, we mainly refer to GIS in relation to 'geographic information system' software through which we produce maps, perform spatial analyses and manipulate and manage data. In our role as planning educators, we have come to accept the fact that it is not universally loved; yet the results of work produced by today's GIS packages have never been more popular, thanks in part to new social media platforms and the ease with which we can exchange maps online. GIS excels as a tool for helping describe our world, and this is a real strength. However, we need to advance two words of warning here. The first is that any map inevitably simplifies the real world, since it will only ever be an abstract representation of it, a snapshot of a place. This is obvious but too often forgotten, so we would be wise to approach all maps, no matter who produces them, with a good degree of caution.

The second word of warning here relates to the fact that it is now almost too easy to point, click and produce a map. We have better GIS software than ever before, more data and therefore we see more maps than ever. This raises the danger of us succumbing to Maslow's so-called 'law of the instrument', described like this: 'I suppose it is tempting, if the only tool you have is a hammer, to treat everything as if it were a nail.' The point here is that the tendency very often is to take data and immediately proceed to making a map, even if it is not the most appropriate way to look at an issue (e.g. if time is a more important variable than space). But, if we can approach with caution, and not 'treat everything as if it were a nail', then GIS as a descriptive tool is unparalleled, particularly in relation to the following:

- Producing thematic maps, such as those that provide an overview of the poverty rate across US counties, or the percentage of people voting for a particular political party, for example.
- Producing zoning and other types of planning-related maps that show land ownership, classification or categorisation (as in Chapter 6).
- Deriving statistics on the geography of places. This could be calculating the area of a country that is, say, pasture land, or it could be calculating how many people live within a specific distance of a location (like an airport). This is covered more in Chapter 7.
- More complex spatial analysis, such as understanding travel flows over a complex network, as looked at in Chapter 8.

Description, we would argue, is a necessary first step on the way to understanding our world, and modern GIS software therefore has a central role to play if we are serious about getting to grips with the world. Yet, as proponents of GIS, we do not think that a complete understanding of the world can be reached with a single approach. It is here that we are also mindful of the words of the famous Dutch systems scientist Edsger Dijkstra, who noted that 'The tools we use have a profound and devious influence on our thinking habits, and therefore on our thinking abilities'.

However, if we are mindful of the partiality of any single route to understanding, particularly in a discipline that is about people and places, and the multiple, complex and contested uses of land, then the power of GIS and spatial analysis is clear. As a tool for describing and representing the geography of our world, GIS software is unsurpassed. The fact that its initial origins are inextricably linked to the management of land, through the late Roger Tomlinson's Canada Land Inventory project (1967), is indicative of the fact that its enduring appeal relates to its utility and simplicity, with the 'layered' approach to geographic data remaining a central feature of all modern GIS software. This last point is important, because in addition to being a tool for description, analysis and management, GIS is also very much a discipline in itself, often referred to as 'geographic information science'. To put it simply, then, not only is there nothing wrong with description but also if we cannot describe the world in detail, our ability to understand it is significantly diminished.

GIScience as a discipline

At the start of this book, it is worthwhile highlighting the fact that 'GIS' is also an important academic discipline in itself, and not simply a tool for understanding and analysis. The existence of academic journals such as the *International Journal of Geographical Information Science* and *Transactions in GIS*, university degree courses in Geographic Information Science, and geographic information science research centres at universities across the world speak to a vibrant global community of geographic data practitioners. Whether people in this discipline self-identify as geographic information scientists, geographic data scientists or some other name not yet in common use, the thing they all have in common is a desire to understand, analyse and help solve problems using a geographic information systems approach. This might be with traditional GIS software methods or, increasingly, with open source and command-line-based tools such as R or Python. No matter what tools we use, and they will inevitably develop and change over time, the foundations of geographic information science remain true.

But what does GIScience actually do? To answer this question, we refer interested readers to *Foundations of Geographic Information Science* (Duckham et al., 2003) in which the authors set out the nature of the field, the importance and value of geographic data and several other important elements to GIScience. For users of GIS in planning and the built environment, such as those reading this book, it is easiest to think about it as follows:

- GIScience is about processing and analysing spatial data (think of this as kind of like the 'dirty work' of GIScience);
- GIScience is a spatial, scientific approach to places and the relationships they have with other places (examples here include commuting and migration);

- GIScience is about developing and improving spatial scientific methods that help us understand important real-world problems (e.g. how concentrated is poverty? How connected are a group of neighbourhoods?);
- GIScience, as the 'science' part suggests, is about taking a replicable, measured approach to understanding the world, using a quantitative spatial approach; and
- GIScience helps develop the theory and tools that we use in geographic information system software and plays a key role in the development of the wider discipline of GIS.

If we are looking for a simple definition of GIScience, then the world's foremost GIS software company provides it, as follows:

> Abbreviation for geographic information science. The field of research that studies the theory and concepts that underpin GIS. It seeks to establish a theoretical basis for the technology and use of GIS, study how concepts from cognitive science and information science might apply to GIS, and investigate how GIS interacts with society.
>
> (ESRI, 2018)

The last point in this quote, about how GIS interacts with society, is an important one because of the potential power GIS has to produce maps and geovisualisations that can inform people, capture imagination, highlight important issues and tell stories, as we discuss in the following sections.

GIS for engagement and communication

Sometimes when we are working on a GIS project, the results might never be shared with others. For example, sometimes it is useful just to explore and assess spatial data in a GIS to check its validity and completeness. But such cases are the exception and most often when working in a GIS environment we will produce results that others will see. Sometimes the purpose of GIS work might actually be for engagement and communication with others.

For example, one of the authors was writing about the important issue of urban population density, since it is a long-standing and important question for planners and built environment professionals. Questions about optimal urban densities are often posed yet are difficult to answer. Therefore, we decided to explore data on the topic for 39 countries across Europe and then attempt to identify the most densely populated 1 km square in each country (Figure 2.1), in order to (1) find the answer to this question, (2) engage others who might be interested and (3) communicate the results with others in an easy-to-understand way. The results were a set of images which highlighted the fact that Spain and France have by far the highest urban densities of any European countries and that many areas we might consider 'densely populated' are in fact not so dense when we compare them with other places in Europe. Example maps from this project are shown in Figure 2.1, for Spain and Sweden.

Figure 2.1   *1 km × 1 km population density visualisations*

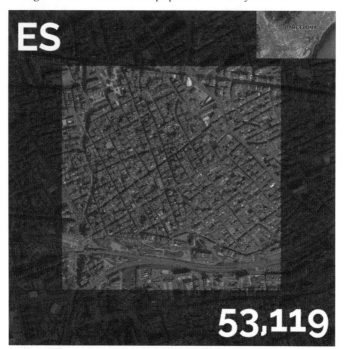

Source: EU GEOSTAT 2011 data mapped by Alasdair Rae

This small project, written up as a short article online, received significant attention and spawned a series of further media pieces looking at the question of density and the historical development of urban centres. It also set off debates about urban issues more generally, and was widely covered in the UK and international media.

We mention this example here because the simple images above were produced using modern GIS software with the aim of public engagement and communication very much in mind, and this, we would argue, is one of the great strengths of contemporary GIS. That is why, in Chapter 5, we go into more depth about the topic of geovisualisation and what it can do for us. Following this, in Chapter 6, we also provide some more practical advice, in recognition of the fact that producing clear, effective maps is not as straightforward as it might seem. But let us be clear here: GIS as a tool for engagement and communication has real power; and in planning and the built environment, where public consultation and engagement play an important role, GIS can be a very effective tool.

On this last point, it would be remiss of us not to highlight the recent emergence of major online mapping platforms, which are already revolutionising our ability to communicate and engage with spatial data. Two prime examples here include CARTO and Mapbox, both powerful geospatial tools in themselves but also highly effective communication platforms that allow users to create online, interactive maps and then share them with the wider world. A good example of this is a project by Córdoba City Council in southern Spain. In fulfilling one of their main objectives of providing information to their citizens in a simple, comprehensive and accessible way, they have used CARTO to visualise important data in the region, as you can see in the screenshot in Figure 2.2 and on the City's website.

Figure 2.2   *CARTO home page*

GIS FOR URBAN PLANNING BY THE CORDOBA CITY COUNCIL

The Urban Municipal Management of the City Council of Cordoba (in Southern Spain), in fulfilling one of the main objectives of providing information to citizens in a simple and comprehensive way, has made use of CARTO to visualize important data of the area. Check out their website to see all the plans and maps available.

Source: CARTO

In a sense, then, new tools like CARTO allow people with no special skills to see what might be planned for their city, where things are happening or how specific areas are zoned. This has the potential to increase citizen participation in planning and, importantly, to give people a voice. Thus, we view communication here very much in the sense of a dialogue rather than a diktat on what the world is like or how it should be.

GIS in education

It is also important that we recognise the important role GIS has in education, not least because this book was written with students in mind. GIS can be thought of as software, it can be understood more specifically as GIScience, and it can be a great tool for engagement and communication; yet it is also a powerful learning tool in itself. Getting to grips with spatial data in a GIS setting can teach us a lot about the world, though perhaps not as much as exploring it on foot and speaking to people. And this is a key point. In an ideal situation, we might wish to get to know the world at close quarters and understand people and places though direct interaction, but this is simply not possible because of the scale and complexity of the world. GIS provides a shortcut to understanding, and is not perfect, but as long as we are aware of its shortcomings we can learn a lot about the world just from using it. In order to demonstrate this, we can refer readers to some examples from our own teaching experience as GIS educators.

If you are a university student who has chosen, or is required, to take a GIS class it is useful to think about GIS in relation to the different approaches we mention above but it is also important to see GIS as a way of learning about the world in itself. This is why, in our own teaching, over a combined two decades, we have attempted to introduce students to the theory and practice of GIS in a way that also helps educate them about the world. That is why in our Geographic Information for Planning practical sessions we ask students to download small area data from the UK census, explore it, map it and report on it; or why in our Open Source GIS class we ask students to download land use and tax plot data for New York City and explore and map it. To put it simply, we think that while we learn about the practicalities of GIS software in relation to where to point and click, it is a missed opportunity if we do not also use it to learn more about the world.

This principle, of GIS as education, is one that we have tried to incorporate into this book as much as possible by using examples from different countries and cities across the world. Although our focus here is on the use of GIS in Higher Education, in recent years there has also been a significant uptake in learning through GIS in primary and secondary education contexts, and this is a great development since it allows much younger students to engage with geographic data in ways that make sense to them. In the context of this book, there are several principal ways in which GIS in education can help us learn:

- Using GIS in an educational context helps us learn about the structure and nature of geographic data and how it is different from non-spatial data;
- Working in an educational environment allows us to experiment, make mistakes, explore interesting avenues and generally take a more interest-led approach to GIS;
- Using GIS in an educational setting allows us to develop our spatial problem-solving skills;
- GIS in educational settings provides an early opportunity to learn about how to deal with 'bad data' (see Chapter 4) and how to handle data more generally, which can be a major challenge for even the most experienced GIS user; and
- Finally, working with GIS in an educational setting helps develop transferable skills because GIS is, by its very nature, an inter- and multidisciplinary discipline that has wide applicability across a range of subjects.

So, we hope readers will understand that using GIS tools is also a great opportunity to learn about the world we live in, to learn about data and to learn skills that are widely transferable, regardless of how software changes in future.

Conclusion

There are many different GIS textbooks aimed at students, some of which attempt to speak to those working in planning and the built environment. Some of these go into great technical detail, whereas others are more broad-brush. In the rest of this book, what we attempt to do is cover what we consider to be the most important elements of GIS for students studying urban or regional planning and related disciplines. As such, we do not attempt comprehensive coverage of GIS as a discipline, or all the potential uses of GIS in practice. What we have tried to do, instead, is provide you with a rounded overview of some of the most important elements if you want to become an effective user of GIS in relation to theory, practice, applications but also limitations.

Beyond the confines of this book, our larger aim is to reinvigorate the use of maps in planning and to motivate the next generation of planning professionals to use GIS more and not to see it as the domain of the specialist. Initially, when GIS software was difficult to use and expensive to obtain, and when data was hard to come by, the notion of the 'GIS specialist' may have made sense, but to us it no longer does. It should be an important tool in the planner's toolbox and it really can help us discover the world anew. It is, we would argue, too important to be left to the specialists!

Chapter 3

GIS: A Spatial Database of Our World

Introduction

Over the past half-century GIS has revolutionised the way that we visualise and analyse our world. It has opened up a world of computer assisted (geo-) graphical exploration, allowing spatial patterns and ordering within social and physical processes to be intuitively grasped and communicated using the power of maps.

But to say that GIS is simply a graphical tool not only underplays its extraordinary power for analysing spatial relations between things, but also ignores the way that it can allow us to reimagine and rework ways of *doing* things. By allowing us to collect, store, manipulate and analyse large quantities of structured information about things on earth, GIS has enabled far-reaching shifts in the way that businesses, citizens and consumers view and find their way around 'their' world.

Take Google. Google has risen to be the world's foremost Internet company by understanding the latent value in information when it can be structured in a way that permits its widespread diffusion and use. Its mission is 'to organize the world's information and make it universally accessible and useful'. Following the acquisition of mapping company Keyhole in October 2004, the Internet giant released its now ubiquitous Google Maps service the following year. The genius behind this move came from the realisation by Google that the maps and satellite imagery, while impressive, were of limited value by themselves; but – as befits their mission – when used as a framework to organise information about everything else and to permit new ways of searching for information, we add a new dimension to the way we can grow and harvest knowledge. That is why 'location services' became the 'killer app' driving innovation and growth in mobile platforms. Put simply, GIS extends our abilities to manage and interrogate vast quantities of structured information into the second, third and even fourth dimensions.

But these innovations depend on the structuring of data: the concept of a *database*. The database is itself based on an idea that is as ancient as human civilisation itself: that organised, structured information is more useful than random information. As Heathcote (2003) puts it, 'a database is a collection of data. ... The word database often now refers to data held on a computer but non-computerised databases also exist' (p. 91). The same information, when

20

stored, classified and ranked, allows it to be quantified and searched much more rapidly than would otherwise be the case.

We believe that, all told, a GIS is a database.

This chapter aims to show that by thinking of GIS as a database we can better understand how analysis can be performed on spatial data, and how applications can be built that harness the unique power of databases to quickly retrieve information. This is a different way to thinking about GIS than starting with the map – indeed, by thinking of GIS as a database we more usually *end up with* the map rather than starting with it. That is because maps are essentially collections of objects; maps impose some sort of order and apply rules on a selection of data about things on earth.

As this chapter will also show, thinking of GIS as a database helps us to understand how spatial data is treated within computer environments: how software applications deal with the problems of storing and working with information that is geographical in nature. We will seek to define and then extend the commonly used database metaphors that we use in our everyday digital lives: for example, the idea of 'records' of things organised into 'fields' of information. These ideas are used in GIS environments, but they are also elaborated on and extended by spatial thinking. Imagine a typical, user-managed database such as a list of contacts stored on a mobile phone. It is natural for us to think about organising our contacts using fields like 'name', 'address', 'phone number' and so on. With GIS we also store *map objects* in the same way: the geographical coordinates of a point describing that person's address within a city, so that it can be displayed on a map. The point – the map object – is essentially another field in the contacts database. The chapter will begin first by defining some basic database concepts before turning its attention to how these concepts fit within a GIS.

At this point, it is then necessary to develop the ideas of *spatial data models* and *attributes*. These are particular ways that information about things is stored within a GIS environment, and they relate to the database way of thinking about the world. They are derived, ultimately, from the techniques that computer scientists created in the earliest computers for storing and retrieving data, but they are still relevant to us now. The second substantive section of the chapter does that.

Finally, the chapter shows how the database way of thinking works practically within common GIS applications and in performing basic GIS tasks. For example, we demonstrate the role of the underlying 'database architecture' in facilitating 'joins' between different datasets and the dynamic links between map views and tabular views of the same dataset.

The importance of structured data

Most computer applications rely on the imposition of highly structured *schemas* in order to be able to work with user-generated data. While it is possible for computers to store random, unstructured collections of information, it is rarely efficient to search or work with these collections. Although there are advances in computing such as the use of Artificial Intelligence or Neural Nets that are designed to mimic more natural, intuitive heuristics in information processing, these have not yet found wide application within GIS, possibly because the very large nature of most spatial databases places a premium on the speed with which operations can be carried out on the data. By and large, the more structured a dataset is, the faster it will be for a computer to process and work with it.

All data in computers is ultimately made up of *bits*, that is, ones and zeroes. These bits are organised into collections, called *bytes*, that can be used to represent single characters within a *character set* (these character sets normally include all the letters of the alphabet, all the digits, common punctuation as well as more specialised characters). It is helpful to know about these character sets and encodings because many GIS tools and programs work very closely with them. The most ubiquitous early character set in computing is called ASCII – the American Standard Code for Information Interchange. ASCII uses one byte to represent any one of its set of 128 characters. ASCII is now a subset of the more expansive UTF character encoding which allows for a much wider range of characters and alphabets used in real-world writing systems, such as Arabic or Hebrew. UTF uses more bytes, and therefore files in UTF-8 tend to be larger and potentially more processor-intensive for computers to deal with. Because of the parsimony it achieves and the premium placed on processing speed, many GIS operations such as the use of spatial analysis tools in ArcGIS, may still use files encoded in ASCII.

Beyond the level of bits and bytes, we start to see collections of data that more closely represent real-world phenomena that we might recognise. Information scientists sometimes refer to this as a *data hierarchy*. If a bit (a single one or zero) is at the bottom of the hierarchy, then a database – an entire, organised collection of data – is at the top. The intermediate levels of the hierarchy contain digital representations of real-world *analogues*, such as pieces of text ('strings'), files and records. Typically, in thinking about information and database concepts, we see a database as containing one or more files, which each in turn contain one or more records. These records are in turn made up of fields containing unique pieces of structured information (such as a string containing part of an address). Figure 3.1 provides an example of a data hierarchy.

Data hierarchies are equally applicable to GIS environments and applications. Different software products use their own proprietary terminology but they all adopt some version of common database concepts to organise spatial data. To demonstrate this, we can take the example of an ESRI Shapefile, one of the most commonly used proprietary spatial data formats. A Shapefile is analogous to a 'file' in the common database hierarchy. It contains a structured set of data about one particular type of thing: rivers, roads, post offices or census tracts, for example. We might refer to these as 'classes' of objects. Now, normally the first instinct in working with a spatial dataset such as a Shapefile is to open it within a GIS to look at it on a map – that is, to preview its map objects. But these map objects are but one representation, and a partial one at that, of the content of the Shapefile.

Imagine a Shapefile called 'Pubs' containing the results of a geographical survey of drinking establishments in a city. A simple way of representing these

Figure 3.1   *Data hierarchy*

Hierarchy	Example
Database	**Affordable housing database** Sites file ← Dwellings file / Tenants file
File	**Dwellings file** <table><tr><td>ID</td><td>Address</td><td>Type</td><td>*etc.*</td></tr><tr><td>00223454</td><td>23 Acacia Avenue</td><td>House</td><td></td></tr><tr><td>00233621</td><td>65b Apple Tree House</td><td>Apartment</td><td></td></tr><tr><td>01288363</td><td>112 Derwent Building</td><td>Studio</td><td></td></tr></table>
Record	**Dwelling record** 00233621 | 65b Apple Tree House | Apartment
Field	**Dwelling field** Address 65b Apple Tree House
Unicode character	**Character** **0x36** (UTF -8 encoding for digit 6)
Byte (8 bits)	**Byte** **00110110** (Bits that make up the byte 0x36)
Bit	**Bit** **0** (First bit of the byte 0x36)

Source: Authors

pubs geographically might be as points on a map. The Shapefile contains map objects: a collection of points each representing one pub. Lying behind these points is a set of structured information about the pubs: the name of the establishment, the owning brewery, the type of establishment, its opening hours, perhaps some flags indicating the presence of attractions like hot food or live music. This information is more often than not represented textually (although note it is entirely possible to store other types of information within structured database environments, including photographs, sound recordings, video, etc.). It is not spatial information per se but it is related to a place on Earth given that it describes something that is spatially located: the pub. Most GIS refer to this sort of information as 'attributes' – this gives the impression that it is subservient to the map object; that this information describes characteristics of the map object. While not inaccurate, that is not necessarily the most helpful way of thinking about the information hierarchy. Indeed, it is entirely possible to think in theoretical terms about this informational relationship being the other way round: that the map object (in this example, the point) describes something (in this example, the location) *about the record.*

Put this way, the map object might be thought of as simply a special type of *field* which exists alongside the other fields in the record. Complications arise because the nature of different GIS software architectures treat this conceptual relationship in various ways. To take two well-known examples:

- The ESRI Shapefile allows only one map *feature* per record. It is represented in tabular form as a special type of field called 'SHAPE'. The existence of the SHAPE field is mandatory, and all records must have an associated map feature (although it can technically be 'null', or empty). Logical integrity is maintained by the stipulation that all map features in a Shapefile must be of the same type (i.e. point, line or polygon). The next chapter contains a discussion of the structure of Shapefiles and why they have the ubiquitous de facto standard for the exchange of vector data within the GIS environment.
- Like the Shapefile, the MapInfo Table only allows one map *object* per record. There is no tabular representation of this object. Unlike the Shapefile, the existence of map objects within a table is optional. Tables may be entirely tabular (just alphanumeric data, no map objects), or they may contain a mix of records with map objects and those without map objects. In this sense, the MapInfo Table reinforces the idea that the spatial object is simply another piece of information *about the record.*

Unique identifiers

The relevance of the database paradigm is further highlighted by the importance of ID numbers within common spatial data formats. It is a common rule of database design that records within a table should be unique. To help reinforce this, most database tables use a system of unique identifiers, sometimes called *primary keys*, to help maintain referential integrity. This is particularly important when tables are joined to other tables (see the section 'Table linkages – joining tables' in this chapter) because the computer must always be clear that it is joining to the right record. Unique identifiers help avoid duplication of data in a database. This is an important consideration when using a database for analysis: if we were using our fictional file of pubs to answer questions like, 'how many pubs are within 500 metres of my house?', then it is important to ensure that there are not spurious duplicates in the file that would lead to incorrect results.

GIS file formats use systems of IDs to identify records within the file. In an ESRI Shapefile, this is often called the FID (or Feature ID). These are used, among other things, to maintain a link within the GIS between the map objects as stored in memory and the tabular data as stored in memory. Most GIS formats adopt a multi-part file structure in which the tabular and geographic data is kept in separate files in the computer's file system. The tabular data may typically be stored by the GIS using a file format like .DBF (see Box 3.1). This is simply for computational expediency and efficiency and should in practical terms be invisible to the analyst, and the multi-part nature of these files only becomes apparent when using the computer's file system to move and copy files.

Box 3.1   What is a DBF?

As microcomputers became more popular in the 1980s the market for semi-professional home and business applications software mushroomed. Along with the markets for word processing and spreadsheets software (led by WordPerfect and Lotus, respectively) there was a major market for database software. The early market leader was Ashton-Tate's dBase, one of the biggest-selling software products of its time. The advantage of dBase was that it allowed a relatively simple way of storing and querying large amounts of structured data in a microcomputer environment at a time when the alternatives were to develop major systems on mainframe computers. Although dBase itself is no longer widely used, the most important legacy of dBase has been the .DBF file format, a convenient format for storing 'flat file' tabular data. As well as being readable by nearly all major analytical software applications (including Microsoft Excel, Microsoft Access, SPSS and so on), it has been widely adopted within GIS to store 'attribute data' alongside geographic data. The ESRI Shapefile format uses a .DBF file as one of three required files. Similarly, .DBF files can be used natively by MapInfo Professional and QGIS among others. The widespread use of the .DBF format means that it is often comparatively easy to examine and edit some of the data held in GIS file formats using other (non-GIS) software like Excel. Nothing lasts forever, though, and while .DBFs remain widely used, software is increasingly turning to other file formats as well, especially open source GIS applications where basic delineated text formats (such as Comma Separated Values – .CSV) are widely used.

Spatial ontologies: ways of representing what exists

In philosophy, ontology is concerned with the existence of being. Knowing when something exists is a fundamental prerequisite in any type of analysis. Practically, this gives rise to the need to define, and seek agreement on, systems that allow us to identify entities and the relationships between them. Consequently, a spatial ontology allows us to communicate with each other and with computer models, including databases, safe in the knowledge that we are all describing the same thing.

This idea is particularly important to conceptualisations of GIS that foreground the importance of databases. Decisions that are made about how to structure a database necessarily involve setting out, or accepting, an ontology – this of course may be explicit or it may be assumed or inferred. Spatial thinking adds its own set of complications to ontology. We might recognise the same idea or concept in different ways (using different spatial representations) dependent on scale. We return to this idea, and its practical significance, later in this chapter. For the time being, when thinking about the design of databases that might underpin a GIS, the importance of ontology lies in the decisions that are taken about how information is represented in the systems of fields, records, data types and categories and so on that are core features of tabular data within computerised information processing environments.

Sometimes decisions that are made about database design leave such an indelible imprint of the underlying ontology that it is impossible to undo later without significant additional data collection and work. For example, if in building a GIS model of the built form in a city the decision is taken to represent residential buildings as *physical* entities rather than *legal* entities, it will be very difficult to later use the database as a basis for storing information about individual flats or apartments. This is because the very idea of an apartment is not recognised in terms of the physical materiality of a building – it is an internal subdivision of space, and sometimes only in the legal sense. In such an ontology, we know a building by virtue of it having walls. It is not a legal construct. A different type of ontology would recognise a building when it had a name, or an address.

The practical implications of ontology within databases become apparent very quickly when working with spatial representations. For example, a parcel of land might have a very widely used and colloquially known name (the 'rec ground' for example). The same parcel of land might have a precise legal definition by virtue of a title deed, with its extents shown on a map (or possibly simply described in text using 'metes and bounds'). Over time, the parcel becomes subdivided. One of the subdivisions is then sold and developed as housing. The remaining part of the field is still known as the 'rec ground', even though it is smaller and its legal definition has changed. Then, the owner of an adjacent field buys the remaining part of the 'rec ground' and removes the physical fences between the two. The colloquial name persists and is eventually applied informally to the whole of the parcel. Time passes, the field is sold again, subdivided again such that the part that was originally a portion of the 'rec ground' is developed for housing. Local people may continue to refer to the unimproved land as the 'rec ground' even though it shares absolutely no common geography with the original 'rec ground'. Designing a spatial ontology – or a database system – that can cope with such complexities is clearly difficult. But this example is not spurious or indeed that uncommon. GIS systems dealing with urban land will be very quickly confronted by the challenges of dealing with systems of representation that are not permanent through time or across space.

The intuitive immediacy of maps, and the widespread availability of GIS tools, can fool us into taking ontological shortcuts without thinking about whether the systems we are putting in place – the record and fields in the database – are actually capable of supporting the analyses we might want to do now or in the future. There are other problems, too. The same type of complacency often leads to us falling into the trap that everything happens 'somewhere', or that we can accurately describe the location of each and every phenomenon. This is often not as easy as it first sounds.

Take the example of crime. The spatial location of crimes is sometimes very obvious, but mostly difficult to pin down precisely. A simple mugging, for example, could reasonably be assigned coordinates in space and time (it happened outside the supermarket at 10.45 pm, for example). A vehicle theft might be equally unproblematic to locate in space – most people know where they left their cars before they were stolen. Other types of crime, for example financial crimes, may not exist in space. They may be the cumulative result of actions over several locations and times. It would not be possible to conceptualise of one place where the crime was committed, or indeed where its impact on victims was felt. A database may, then, simply record the location of the perpetrator's abode. Equally, some crimes may change over time: think of a serious assault which later becomes a murder when the victim succumbs to their injuries at a later date. It is not known where or when the assault took place, although it is known where the victim was found and also where they subsequently died. The question, in all cases, is: How best to represent these instantiations of a crime in a database? What is a crime? *Where* do crimes happen? These questions are superficially easy to answer, but it is more difficult to pin down the answers precisely.

This leads to the idea of representing uncertainty in spatial databases. One of the significant drawbacks of numerical systems is that it is impossible to know if a value is precise or rounded. If the length of a road is recorded in a database as 10 km, is it exactly 10 km or *about* 10 km? We might be able to tell if we look at other entries in the database: if they all seem to be rounded to the nearest kilometre then we would be pretty confident in saying that the road is about 10 km long, but may not be exactly 10 km long.

Some systems use formal methods of recording uncertainty, especially with regards to the spatial location of objects represented within databases. In the UK, the Royal Mail's Postal Address File (PAF) contains a list of every address – or 'delivery point' – known to the postal service. Coordinates allow this data to be mapped within GIS. The principle is that the coordinates should refer to the location where the mail is delivered: the postbox or letterbox at the front door in most cases. Clearly such a level of accuracy may be hard to achieve in practice. A system of Positional Quality Indicators (PQIs) is used to provide users with an indication of the extent to which they might rely on the accuracy of the spatial attributes in the dataset (see Box 3.2).

Box 3.2   Example of positional quality indicators used in UK address data

PQI	Description of ADDRESS-POINT data
10	Within the building of the matched address closest to the postcode mean determined automatically by Ordnance Survey or Ordnance Survey of Northern Ireland (OSNI) (BT® postcode area only).
20	As above, but determined to visual inspection by GROS (General Register Office for Scotland).
30	Approximate to within 50 m of true position (postcodes relating to developing sites may be within 100 m of true position).
40	The mean of the positions of addresses previously matched in ADDRESS-POINT but which have subsequently been deleted or recoded (very rarely used).

$\rightarrow$

50	Estimated position based on surrounding postcode coordinates, usually to 100 m resolution, but 10 m in Scotland.
60	Postcode sector mean (direct copy from ADDRESS-POINT). See glossary for additional information.
90	No coordinates available.

Source: http://digimap.edina.ac.uk/webhelp/os/data_files/os_manuals/codepoint_v2.1.pdf

Place names often present particular challenges. Often we will know generally where is being referred to by a place name, but a more precise reading will be usually aided by context. For example, Manchester may refer to the Manchester 'city region', or Greater Manchester, the City of Manchester, or the 'M' postcode area, or any number of dozens of less formal senses of what and where 'Manchester' is. If we refer to 'the City' (with a capital 'C'), we might not be referring to the City of London as a spatial construct but as an institutional construct. Some well-known place names might not exist at all formally, or may have changed in their meaning. For example, the city centre of Stoke-on-Trent does not technically exist – the de facto commercial centre of the city of Stoke-on-Trent is the town of Hanley, while Stoke-on-Trent is a neighbouring town that gave its name to a new confederation of towns formed into a city in the nineteenth century.

The world as a model

Scale

A very important part of the context for understanding spatial ontologies, and their practical implications for database design, can be found in spatial scale. At the simplest level, the spatial scale of analytical interest drives decisions about the accuracy that might be required in a spatial database, or choices about the type of features used to represent objects on a map. A spatial database of National Health Service facilities might reasonably record only the name of the administrative area (e.g. a ward) in which the facility is located. Either the polygon representing the ward boundary or a point representing its spatial centre (*centroid*) may become the objects that represent a health care facility. These would work fine for analysis at the national scale: how does the density of hospital beds per inhabitant vary across an entire country, for example. For more local analysis, a crude system of geographic locations such as that described above would be of little use. An analysis, for example, of the proportion of the population that lives within a 1 km walk of a primary health care facility would require those facilities to be mapped to a much higher level of precision (see Box 3.3 for a comparison between precision and accuracy). For large facilities, such as hospitals, it may be necessary to understand that they have separate entrances and to map these accordingly. Again, the scale of the analysis drives decisions about the scale of the data and the representation of the objects within the database.

More sophisticated spatial databases may have more than one spatial representation of objects within any given ontology. For example, imagine a spatial database containing information on housing developments within the management of a landlord. The main database table, *developments*, contains information on the individual developments. This links to further attribute tables on either a one-to-one or a one-to-many basis. For example, information on individual properties (e.g. flats) within each development might exploit a one-to-many relationship. Each record in the *developments* table is also linked to several spatial layers: a polygon layer which has detailed building outlines for each development; another polygon layer which has detailed boundaries (curtilages) for the site; and a point layer representing the address location of the scheme's management office.

Within such a database, all the tables are related to each other on the basis of a unique development ID. Different spatial representations of the data could be used depending on the scale of the analysis and the type of question being asked: for example, an analysis of the total land area in management would rely on the curtilages layer; a calculation of gross residential density might use the building outlines coupled with information on the number of residential units; a logistics routing analysis for management vehicles (e.g. for repairs) might use the layer of the location of the management offices, and so on.

Box 3.3   Precision versus accuracy

Two concepts that are often confused are precision and accuracy. Precision and accuracy both have quite specific meanings within GIS. Precision refers to the distance between a representation of something and its real location. A highly precise map layer will generally depict objects very close to their actual location. As such, there is a relationship between scale and precision: the larger the map scale (the finer the resolution), the more precise we would normally expect the representation to be. The same goes for data collection: a GPS receiver capable of producing a fix to the nearest 1 m would lead to more precise data than one producing fixes to the nearest 10 m.

Accuracy, on the other hand, relates to the systematic fit that the data has to the actual location. Some sort of systematic error introduced into data collection (e.g. a GPS receiver was faulty) would affect accuracy even if the data remained highly precise.

These two concepts are often visualised using a 'target' metaphor. High levels of precision can yield objects that are closely grouped together (as in A) but yet their accuracy can be low (as in B). Accurate data, on the other hand, can be imprecise (as in C). Worst of all, data may be neither accurate nor precise (as in D).

It is worth noting that the scientific definition of precision and accuracy is slightly different. As laid down by the International Organization for

$\rightarrow$

Standardization (ISO), 'accuracy' refers both to precision and to the idea of 'trueness'. 'Trueness' is closer to the idea of 'accuracy' as used in the GIS literature. Highly accurate data, according to the ISO, is both precise and 'true'.

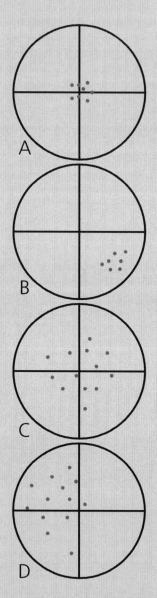

Source: Figure taken from http://www.gislounge.com/gis-data-a-look-at-accuracy-precision-and-types-of-errors/

Generalisation

It is often expedient to sacrifice precision. In an ideal world, however, we would retain accuracy at all times. Highly precise data often requires significant storage capacity and computational power – sometimes as a result of the level of numerical precision (e.g. number of decimal places – see Table 3.1) required to store coordinates, and sometimes as a result of the number of coordinates stored. A highly precise dataset of road centre lines may be made up of many hundreds of vertices to describe the course of a single road link. At a large scale, each coordinate pair describing each vertex may require a high level of numerical precision.

Sometimes this degree of precision is important. But at other times, it can be a hindrance. As a rule in mapping or modelling physical or natural phenomena, precision is valued; but for maps of socioeconomic data, *geographic* precision may be less important (although the precision of the underlying attribute data – for example, unemployment statistics – would remain equally important). Mapping the precise boundaries of statistical geographic units such as Census tracts or 'output areas' may simply introduce needless cartographic complexity to a map and, worse still, might involve needlessly large file sizes or processing times. That is why it is often desirable to work with 'generalised' map data.

A generalised dataset is one where the precision of the objects has been purposely downgraded. An analyst might choose to generalise a spatial dataset (or to use an already-generalised dataset) for a number of reasons.

Table 3.1   *Spurious levels of precision*

Decimal Places	Actual Distance	Say What?
6	10 centimetres	Your footprint, if you were standing on the toes of one foot.
7	1.0 centimetre	A watermelon seed.
8	1.0 millimetre	The width of paperclip wire.
9	0.1 millimetre	The width of a strand of hair.
10	10 microns	A speck of pollen.
11	1.0 micron	A piece of cigarette smoke.
12	0.1 micron	You're doing virus-level mapping at this point.
13	10 nanometres	Does it matter how big this is?
14	1.0 nanometre	Your fingernail grows about this far in one second.
15	0.1 nanometre	An atom. An atom! What are you mapping?

Source: John Nelson (2013) Silly Geographic Precision (blog post) http://uxblog.idvsolutions.com/2013/11/silly-geographic-precision.html

1. The extent of the analysis is such that processing speed and disk space requirements would be greatly reduced. For example, a government department concerned with mapping a neighbourhood level index of social conditions across an entire country – such as England's Indices of Multiple Deprivation (IMD) – would require boundaries of very small geographic units across a very large area. The purpose of the analysis is not dependent on knowing the precise course of those boundaries; an approximation would suffice. Table 3.2 demonstrates the disk space and processing overheads that can potentially be saved by using generalised versions of a dataset.
2. To enable high speed delivery of data using web mapping platforms.
3. Keeping a high level of precision may not be suitable for shared data. For example, data protection principles might be transgressed if the fully precise dataset was released or displayed in the public domain. Singleton et al. (2011) demonstrate how a set of school catchment areas derived from precise, address level point data had to be generalised to avoid the disclosure of individuals' home addresses.
4. To provide a low-cost version of a dataset. For example, a commercial data provider may choose to provide a generalised version of their data free of charge or at a lower cost, for example to allow the required features to be selected in anticipation of purchase of the full version for a specific study area.

Generalisation functions are available within most GIS packages, either as part of the core toolset or as part of optional extensions or plugins. MapInfo Professional tends to use the term 'simplification' and is a built-in command. ArcGIS provides an extensive suite of tools for generalisation, but these may depend on purchased options. (The full selection of tools for cartographic generalisation require an advanced licence, for example.) QGIS provides similar tools within the Simplify Geometries menu. Free online tools, such as MapShaper (www.mapshaper.org), can also be used.

Table 3.2   *Comparison of generalised versions of Shapefile of English LSOAs 2011*

Version	Compressed file size (zip compression)	Unzipped file size on disk	Total number of vertices
Full	205 MB	483 MB	31,006,405
Generalised	92 MB	131 MB	7,930,253
Clipped and Generalised	23 MB	39 MB	1,892,578
Clipped and Super-Generalised	6 MB	16 MB	398,325

Source: Authors' comparison of files downloaded from UK Data Archive Census Support website.

Regardless of the specific implementation details, most GIS systems employ a variant of the Douglas–Peucker algorithm (Douglas and Peucker, 1973), a recursive mathematical procedure which divides line segments and decides which vertices to keep based on distance from the original line and input parameters such as a maximum distance or tolerance. The result is a best fit approximation of the original line (or polygon boundary) but with a reduced number of vertices (see Figure 3.2). The exact number of vertices lost depends on the tolerance specified. In addition, most systems allow the user to enforce topological integrity – in other words, to retain the key connections with other map objects. This is especially important in the case of lines crossing other lines (e.g. in a dataset of roads) where the generalised features need to keep vertices that are coincident with junctions. It is also of vital importance when generalising a set of contiguous boundaries – such as with administrative or electoral areas – in order to ensure that the parts of boundaries shared by adjacent polygons are generalised in the same way. Figure 3.3 demonstrates the importance of maintaining topological integrity.

Of course, while generalisation has clear benefits for processing speed and cartographic parsimony, it must be remembered that analysis performed on a generalised dataset may be fundamentally affected. A generalised set of polygons will yield less precise geometric calculations, such as

Figure 3.2 *Berwick-upon-Tweed LSOAs: the impact of generalisation*

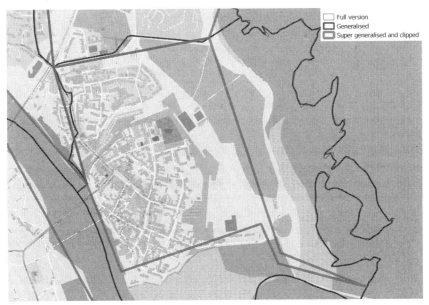

Source: Authors. Data sources: LSOA boundaries, ONS © Crown Copyright; background map, OpenStreetMap.

Figure 3.3   *The effect of polygon generalisation (a) before, (b) after, (c) after but retaining topological integrity*

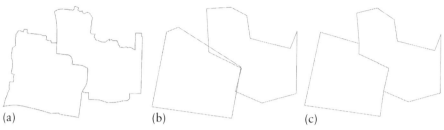

(a)   (b)   (c)

Source: Authors. Data source: LSOA boundaries, ONS.

estimates of area or line length. An analysis of road distances performed using a highly generalised dataset will, by definition, underestimate actual length since the curves in the road – an essential feature – will have been simplified away.

This tendency for generalised lines to be shorter than the real phenomena they represent gives rise to another challenge for the GIS user: What is the appropriate level of generalisation to use? As should be evident from the LSOA examples above, this question can often be answered intuitively. It is obvious that the highly generalised examples are simply too simplistic to be used, for example to determine which streets and properties fall within a specific LSOA and which do not. Equally, they are unlikely to yield accurate geometric calculations, such as of area or perimeter length. This invokes that famous geographical trick question: What is the length of the British coastline? In part, the answer to this depends on definition: What is Britain? What is 'the coast'? But assuming we have certainty about these basic concepts, the question still remains: What is its length?

That's easy, you might say. But think about it a little more. If we did not have the benefit of remote data such as a satellite image, we might be tempted to use existing maps of the coast to help us answer. But the answer, so derived, would simply be a function of the scale of the maps we chose. More detailed maps, which charted every little fissure and inlet and cove, would obviously yield a larger estimate of length: perhaps very significantly larger. This is the *coastline paradox*, and is related to the mathematics of generalisation and *fractals*. A fractal is a pattern that repeats infinitely at whichever scale we choose. At ever larger scales (i.e. as we 'zoom in') yet more detail is revealed. The coastline is an example of something that has near-fractal properties. The closer we look, the more detail we can observe and, as such, any measurement of the length of the coastline depends on *how we measure it* (see Box 3.4 for a particularly interesting example of this). And so it is with nearly every data consideration within GIS: what we do depends on how we measure it – and how we measure it depends on what we want to do with the resulting analysis.

Box 3.4   The curious case of generalisation and the Austrian parliament

Interestingly, the reverse of the phenomenon that generalised lines will tend to underestimate true length can be exploited to purposely *exaggerate* distances. A cartographer named Christoph Schrahe revealed, using a GIS analysis (Schrahe, 2015), that many ski resort managers manipulate data on the length of ski runs by simulating the zig-zag route that a skier might realistically take (assuming that they are not champion alpine ski racer Franz Klammer) rather than measuring the length of the piste's centre line. The findings (and the scale of the exaggeration implied) were of sufficient gravity that the Austrian parliament debated the issue, demonstrating not only the materiality of what might be otherwise dismissed as technical pedantry, but also the ability of GIS to help provide new, objective insights into spatial problems.

 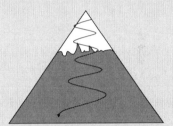

| Most direct route down a mountain: the only true measure of distance, and the route favoured by Franz Klammer. | Route taken down mountain by most mere mortals, and conveniently used by ski resorts to measure piste length. |

Practical database considerations

The final section of this chapter considers the key practical applications of 'database thinking' within GIS systems. As this chapter has introduced, and Chapter 5 will elaborate, data is the key input and, to a large extent, data considerations determine the quality and reliability of the answers we get from the spatial models and processes we build.

The section considers three key database practices within GIS:

- Table design, editing and cleaning
- Table linkages ('joins')
- Abstracting, combining and summarising data

Table design and editing

In GIS we mostly work with data others have provided to us, whether as part of a corporate spatial database or in the form of datasets accessed on and downloaded from the Internet. This gives rise to the first challenge for the analyst: getting the data into a format amenable to the analyses to be performed.

Sometimes this is as simple as making sure the data is in a format that the GIS software can open. As discussed earlier (see also Chapter 5), several computer data formats have come to be recognised as de facto standards: these include the dBase file for tabular data (although equally common are various delimited text standards such as Comma Separated Values, or CSV files); and Shapefiles for vector geographic data. If we come across an exotic file format that the GIS won't read, the first task is to convert it.

The conversion of file formats used to be a job for expensive proprietary software and, to some extent, this is still the case. Good software should be capable of reading and writing a variety of appropriate file formats, and doing so while respecting implicitly the technical standards for that file format. Microsoft Excel, while suffering from some limitations, is pretty good at this: its Open and Save As commands allow the user to select from a very large range of common (and sometimes now largely historic) file formats for the interchange of tabular data. But its limitations are not trivial, especially for the GIS analyst. The main limitation is the maximum number of records (rows) that Excel can handle: standard 32-bit installations of Excel can handle 65,536 rows or, if using Excel 2010 or higher and the newer .XLSX file format, 1,048,576 rows. The former is not enough to successfully load data from NYC's tax lot database, MapPLUTO (about 90,000 records), and the newer format is not enough for a table containing every postcode in the UK (approximately 1.75 million). An annoying recent limitation is the decision by Microsoft to remove the dBase format from the list of file types that it can save to (although mercifully Excel can still open and view dBase files). For bigger jobs, Microsoft Access can sometimes be valuable as it provides a comprehensive set of options for working with text-based files (like CSVs), as well as dBase, Excel and other formats. Proprietary solutions to file format conversion problems include Safe Software's FME suite, a cut-down version of which has been an invaluable and popular component of MapInfo Professional for many years. Many GIS packages – including ArcGIS and MapInfo – will allow connections to be made to existing databases using ODBC (Open Database Connectivity), but more often than not the data transfer is one-way only and it can be very difficult to get ODBC working properly, especially on computers that do not enjoy full administrator access. There are also a growing number of cloud-based file conversion services, both paid-for and free.

It is vitally important to get data 'into shape' before attempting to work with it in a GIS environment. This is usually best done outside the GIS environment, because GIS software typically offers only limited tools for working with tabular data and they are often clunky and difficult to use in comparison with the 'drag and drop' methods that software like Excel provides. At a minimum, getting data into shape means ensuring that the data structure is clear and applied uniformly. Tables in database and GIS software are mostly of the 'flat file' variety, which means that they have rows of data organised into 'fields' (or columns). The table has a heading row which provides the field name for each field (see Table 3.3). This is usually in a shortened form and avoids the use of spaces and other characters that GIS systems often find problematic.

Often the first task is to strip out extraneous information from files, for example by removing redundant header rows which might contain 'metadata'

Table 3.3 *An example 'flat file' table (with fictitious data)*

ID	Cust_Inits	Cust_Surname	Postcode	Email
155244352	EV	Aranovich	AB1 3DF	evaran23@yahoot.com
172663524	A	Jones	B13 9SV	ajonesey2888@tepidmail.com
193884773	R	Singh	EC1V 2UY	singhrd_ltd@geemail.com
...				

(i.e. information about the data file itself). Tables produced by public web portals often contain metadata in the form of additional rows, such as table descriptors or footnotes; these all need to be removed before the file can be used successfully in a GIS. Figure 3.4 shows an example of a typical table extracted from the UK's *Neighbourhood Statistics* website, first as it is downloaded and second as it needs to be to use it within a GIS. Note in particular:

- The removal of extraneous rows (such as table information) to leave only one header rows containing variable names
- The removal of extraneous columns (containing variables not needed in the analysis)
- The renaming of the file for brevity, to remove any illegal characters such as spaces or punctuation (other than the underscore character '_'), and to ensure it does not start with a number
- The renaming of the worksheet or table name to exclude illegal characters
- The provision of shortened variable names which do not include illegal characters

GIS applications can be particularly pernickety about file names, table names and variable names. Limitations often go back to the earliest computing operating systems, when the length of file names and variables were heavily restricted by the file systems of the day – for example, to 8 or 10 characters. What catches most people out is the inclusion of so-called 'illegal characters' – these are symbols, punctuation, non-alphanumeric characters (including accented characters) and even the innocuous space. Always look closely for spaces in file names, table names and variable names, and replace these punctiliously with underscores ('_'). The underscore is the only symbol that you can be confident will not cause computer software any problems. Rogue spaces and other illegal characters are often to blame for unexpected behaviour or failed operations in GIS software. ArcGIS, for instance, will routinely fail to link tables to maps properly if any of its variable and file naming conventions are broken; unhelpfully, it will often do this without any error message to the user.

Once a file has been prepared properly, it should be saved as a separate copy in a file format acceptable to the GIS application you intend to use. Basic

Figure 3.4   *Preparing a table for use in GIS: before (top) and after (bottom)*

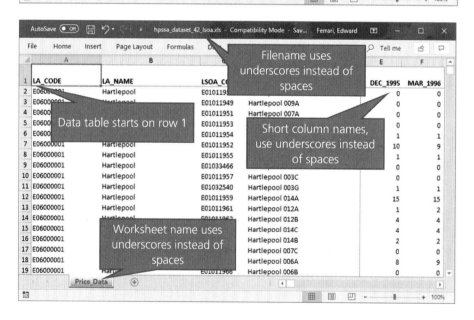

text-based formats like .CSV are the most universally accepted and will usually pose the fewest problems.

Table linkages – joining tables

To minimise disk space and processor overheads, the conventions of database design usually seek to keep the number of fields (columns) in a flat file to a reasonable minimum – often limiting them to the fields that are strictly necessary to uniquely identify the objects in the database. (In relational database terminology, this is called 'normalising' the database.) In the example in Table 3.4 individual customers are the unique objects. Apart from some basic information to permit identification and communication (name, postcode, email address), the table contains nothing other than a unique key (ID number). This unique key and the other pieces of information would be used to link to other tables should there be a need to store additional information about the object. This can be very important when dealing with spatial information, which can be very costly in terms of disk space and processing time. So, rather than store map objects in this table, the database might contain a separate table containing spatial information to which this table is linked (or 'joined').

The example in Table 3.4 enjoys a logical relationship with the example in Table 3.3: the postcode can be used to link the two tables. Each postcode in the Postcode field in Table 3.3 should have a corresponding record in Table 3.4, allowing further information about that postcode to be stored. In this example, taken from a retailing analysis application, postcodes contain information about the Post Town (which can be used to sort direct mail), information on which delivery depot routinely handles deliveries to that postcode, as well as coordinates that have been used to map the approximate location of the postcode.

This is an example of a *many-to-one join* between these two tables, more correctly referred to by database programmers as a *left join* because all of the records in the 'left' (first) table are retained, and matches from the right (second) table are joined to them. Many customer records may link to only one postcode record (if, for example, there is more than one customer living at a postcode). Full Relational Database Management Systems (RDBMSs) allow for a wide range of different types of join, including the full implementation of joins permitted by Structured Query Language (SQL) standards. In practice, though, most GIS systems offer just a basic subset of these joins and it usually requires complex *schemas* to be built to describe the relationships between different tables using standard *left joins*.

Understanding the concept of a table join is fundamental in all GIS packages, although they may be handled in slightly different ways. At the most basic level, GIS usually employs the join concept to relate tabular data in

Table 3.4   *Example flat file: details of postcode and associated fictitious delivery depots*

Shape	FID	Postcode	Posttown	Delivery_Depot	X_coord	Y_coord
Point	234	AB1 3DF	Aberdeen	SCO_12		
Point	235	AB1 3DG	Aberdeen	SCO_12		
...						
Point	236	B13 9SV	Birmingham	WM_01		

Figure 3.5   *Diagram showing 'join' relationship between a data table and an attribute table*

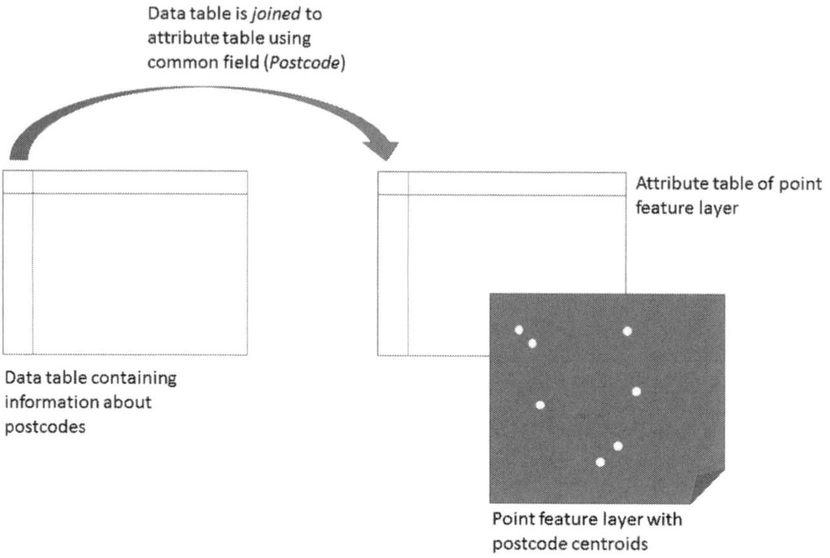

Data table is *joined* to attribute table using common field (*Postcode*)

Attribute table of point feature layer

Data table containing information about postcodes

Point feature layer with postcode centroids

one file to a corresponding set of map objects in another. So, for example, in the postcodes examples in Table 3.4, the user might have a corresponding Shapefile containing point features describing the centroid (geometric centre) of the postcode. To enable a thematic map to be produced that symbolises those points (e.g. by colouring them) according to one of the attributes in the data table (such as *Delivery_Depot*), the two files need to be joined as in Figure 3.5.

Once table joins have been specified in a GIS these are normally kept in memory or the active workspace. This means that the joins will be recreated next time the user opens the workspace, but that the combined (joined) data file is not normally stored as part of the workspace. This keeps disk usage to a minimum, although software settings might be available that allow cached versions of the joined dataset to be retained in the workspace. In ArcGIS, the joins are recreated when the ArcMap Document (.mxd) file is opened. In MapInfo, joins are stored as 'queries' – tables that result from the execution of SQL queries – and these queries are recreated when the use opens a MapInfo Workspace (.wor) which has defined queries.

The tables that result from joins are usually treated by GIS software as tables in their own right although they exist only 'virtually'. With a few exceptions, this means that users are normally free to do operations on or using those tables as they would any other. Operations that would affect the original tables on which the join is based (such as changing table structures or field names) may be restricted, although in some instances edits that are made to the attributes within joined tables will be cascaded back to the original source tables. If building GIS workspaces or applications that rely heavily on joined tables and which may be subject to frequent data editing, it will be important to learn in some detail how the GIS software handles joined tables and what editing restrictions might be imposed.

Combining and summarising data

The final database practice considered in this chapter is that of combining and summarising data within a table. Database query languages like SQL provide a set of tools that allow summaries of data within tables to be produced. Such summaries may be required (or implied) in the process of joins (see previous section of this chapter). If a *many-to-one* join is created, the GIS may need to know how to *aggregate* the many records that might be joined to a single key record. If numeric data is involved, this will normally require some form of calculation (e.g. the calculation of an average value). An example may help: imagine you have a database of information on stores owned by a major multiple retailer. There are two 'flat file' tables. One contains details of individual stores with some basic attributes: floor space in square metres, annual turnover and the name of the county in which the store is located. The other table contains details of counties with some basic socioeconomic and demographic variables: population by socioeconomic group, age profile and so on. The analyst wishes to calculate some basic statistics about store performance by county. The store table would be joined to the county table on the basis of the county name (see Figure 3.6).

When specifying the join, the GIS would ask what should happen to the data in the table with the 'many' records when it is 'collapsed' to single records. A selection of 'aggregate functions' are provided for this purpose which allow the user to specify an appropriate way of aggregating values on a field-by-field basis. Table 3.5 provides an example of the commonly used aggregate functions within GIS.

These aggregate functions are very helpful not only for dealing with one-to-many joins, but also for summarising data within a single table. As with spreadsheet and database applications, a good GIS will allow single variables

Figure 3.6 *One-to-many join*

County_name	Population	Age_60over
Aberdeenshire	234,900	61,000
Berkshire	863,800	161,500
Cheshire	1,028,600	181,600
...		

Store	County	Turnover_GBP
Banchory	Aberdeenshire	£724,000
Oracle Centre 1	Berkshire	£5,233,000
Oracle Centre 2	Berkshire	£3,353,000
Cheshire Oaks	Cheshire	£4,022,000
Macclesfield Centre	Cheshire	£1,342,000

Table 3.5   *Example of common aggregate functions*

Aggregate function	Description	Example for records where County = 'Berkshire'
First	The first matching record is used	For field 'Store', 'Oracle Centre 1' is the first match
Last	The last matching record is used	For field 'Store', 'Oracle Centre 2' is the last match
Sum	The sum of a variable on all matching records is used	For field 'Turnover_GBP', the sum of matching records is £8,586,000 (sum of £5,233,000 and £3,353,000)
Count	The number of matching records is used	For all fields, the count would be 2 records
Average	The arithmetic mean of a variable in all matching records is used	For field 'Turnover_GBP', the average of matching records is £4,293,000 (average of £5,233,000 and £3,353,000)
Max	The maximum value of a variable in all matching records is used	For field 'Turnover_GBP', the maximum is £5,233,000
Min	The minimum value of a variable in all matching records is used	For field 'Turnover_GBP', the minimum is £3,353,000

to be summarised across all records, or by groups of records. In ArcGIS, for example, right-clicking on a column within an attribute table will allow summary groups to be created on the basis of values in that column: the user is then asked to specify how the other variables in the table should be aggregated (using the types of aggregate functions discussed above), before a new summary table is produced.

Conclusion

This chapter conceptualises GIS as a type of spatially enabled database. It argues that a good understanding of basic database concepts allows users to get the most out of GIS applications' capabilities for the management and analysis of data, both spatial and tabular. The case is made for understanding how data is organised and stored within hierarchical database structures. The database heritage of many GIS applications, operations and file formats is described. The importance of 'ontology' – understanding representations of things – is discussed, borrowing heavily from database and computer science. This involves an understanding of related issues including positional accuracy and generalisation. Key concepts that open up huge possibilities for data linkage and analysis within GIS environments include the idea of 'joins' between tables, and the ability to summarise tabular information.

So, if, as we said at the outset of this chapter, a GIS is basically a database that means that data is its lifeblood, how we source, work with and analyse data is a key determinant of our success in using GIS to understand more and communicate better. The next chapter of this book deals with this by looking at what we call the 'currency of GIS': data.

Chapter 4

The Currency of GIS

Introduction

During the past few years we have witnessed a huge increase in the availability of spatial datasets which we can use in a GIS. Examples include New York City's highly detailed MapPLUTO tax lot dataset, the City of Amsterdam's fantastic open geodata resources and comprehensive national mapping products from Ordnance Survey in Great Britain. Such developments have opened up a whole new world of possibilities and they have arisen at a time of significant user growth and technical development in the geospatial world, in large part thanks to the development of open source software like QGIS and R. The question now, of course, is what we can and should do with such data. It is tempting to fire up your GIS and then throw lots of data at it, but we recommend a more measured approach. In this chapter, therefore, we are guided by the following question: 'if data is the currency of GIS, how should we spend it?'

To begin to answer this question systematically we first of all need to think about the role of data within the field of GIScience more broadly, if we want to understand its value; so the next section looks at this issue in more detail. This is done by positioning data within the well-known data–information–knowledge–wisdom (DIKW) hierarchy. We need to understand what data is, and what it can and cannot be used for, if we are to undertake meaningful GIS analysis in the built environment. Fundamentally, we see data as having two roles within GIS. The first is to help us answer questions; the second is to help identify new ones.

The subsequent section delves more deeply into the DIKW hierarchy and uses real-world examples to help show that the opening up of new datasets – often held up as exemplary practice – is only the beginning. Yes, it is okay to get excited about new data sources, but the analytical skill of the user becomes even more important as the contemporary data deluge continues. Contrary to predictions that the data deluge will lead to the end of theory, we believe that, more than ever, careful thought is needed if we are to undertake meaningful analyses.

After looking at the role of data in its wider context, we then move to the more practical issue of data types and formats. This necessarily involves making distinctions between the vector and raster data models in GIS, but here we also get more technical to consider specific file types since they are, after all, a mainstay of the discipline. The longevity of the ESRI Shapefile format is explained here, in addition to its technical specification. This is not perhaps the stuff of dinner party conversation, but in the world of GIS it is very important! We also discuss newer data standards which have become popular in web-based applications, such as GeoJSON and KML.

Moving on from data types and formats, we then turn to look at the subject of 'open' and 'big' data – two buzzwords which have recently risen to prominence. 'Open data' has come to the fore in recent years as governments across the world have sought to demonstrate their transparency and accountability. But all is not what it seems, so we view the open data movement with some caution, while at the same time remaining grateful for the analytical opportunities new datasets open up. However, it is very important to remember here that open data does not equal open knowledge.

The same is true of 'big data'. While we welcome the possibilities created by the availability of massive new datasets, we think that the ubiquity of the term, arguments about volume and claims about its inherent economic value are something of a distraction. Yes, it is certainly true that we can begin to tackle old problems in new ways and that we can mine massive datasets to obtain important insights on global problems, but this does not need to be at the expense of established methods. We believe that 'big data' and 'small data' should be complementary rather than adversarial. This position is similar to the conclusions reached by David Lazer and colleagues (2014) in their study of the Google Flu Trends project, which sought to predict future flu outbreaks using Google search data.

Beyond these two more glamorous data types, we then move to discuss a more important data 'type' encountered by all serious GIS users: 'bad data'. This refers to data that is simply wrong in some way (error), or to data that is incomplete, badly structured, poorly formatted or otherwise impossible to use without further work. Understanding how to deal with these issues is a big part of being a successful GIS analyst, though probably not the most glamorous part!

Finally, we draw the chapter to a close by discussing whether we can ever really expect to progress from data to wisdom in GIS and whether, more philosophically, this is what we should expect in the first place. In doing so, we reflect on the wider academic literature and refer to examples from professional GIS practice.

What is the role of data in GIS?

Perhaps the best starting point for thinking about the role of data in GIS is to take it away and consider where we would be without it. If we had no data, we would not have much use for our GIS software and no analysis would be possible. When we add data, GIS comes to life and we can then begin to understand spatial relationships, develop research questions, map areas of interest and attempt a multitude of other tasks. We can also share data, create new data, quality-test data and, if we are not careful, lose data. Data therefore has a pivotal role to play in the world of GIS, but it is no use on its own: in the world of GIS, data is interdependent. We also need the other component parts of GIS, as identified most famously by Longley and colleagues (2015) as hardware, software, people, procedures and networks. But, before going any further, let's consider what data actually is.

Box 4.1   What is data?

A good way to think about data is to consider it as contextless numbers. Let's take –4.78 and 37.89 as examples. These numbers represent raw numerical data and on their own they have virtually no meaning. We can tell that one is larger than the other, but that is about it. Without context, they are just numbers. Another example would be 175.22 and –37.89. This is also a small number set without any context and at this stage only represents data. But if we tell you that the first pair of numbers are the x and y coordinates of Córdoba in Spain and that the second pair of numbers represent the x and y coordinates of Hamilton, New Zealand we take the numbers out of the domain of data (raw and unstructured) and into information. By telling you that the numbers represent points on the earth, they are now imbued with meaning and therefore become information. If we know a little bit about the earth, we would then be able to say that, based on their latitudes, one is in the northern hemisphere (Córdoba) and one is in the south (Hamilton). This represents knowledge, derived from information. The question of what you should do with such knowledge would be pertinent if you were going to either of these places on holiday. For example, if you were going to Córdoba in the summer then, based on its latitude, it would be wise to pack some light clothing. Note that this step requires some additional external knowledge. We use such an example here because it is very rarely the case that one would travel from data to wisdom without relying on some form of existing knowledge. Data may exist independently of context in the form of raw numbers, but knowledge certainly does not. An additional interesting fact here is that the cities mentioned are almost exact antipodes – if it were possible to tunnel straight through the centre of the earth from Córdoba you would eventually emerge in Hamilton. But anyone with an ounce of wisdom would not even try.

Of course, what we have described so far is technically true, but it is not necessarily how we talk about data or use data in the real world of GIS – and definitely not when using GIS for urban planning in the built environment. This can be a cause for confusion, since the 'data' we use in a GIS *is* typically imbued with meaning. We may import a raw CSV file with a long list of coordinate pairs that we want to plot on a map, but more often we will add data to our GIS that has already been structured, processed and given meaning by a third party.

An excellent example of this is New York City's MapPLUTO dataset, released by the Department of City Planning to meet the growing need for extensive land use and geographic data at the tax lot level in PC mapping format. The 'PLUTO' part of the name stands for Primary Land Use Tax Lot Output and the map bit refers to the version of the dataset in its spatial format. There is also a non-spatial PLUTO version. But what is it? Essentially, it is a land use dataset at the level of 'tax lots', small subdivisions of land covering New York City's five Boroughs. The data is published in the ESRI Shapefile format on a Borough-by-Borough basis, since they are each very large files. Every tax lot record relates to an area on the ground and is associated with a large number of attributes, such as land use, year built, number of floors and many, many more. A detailed description of the dataset is contained in the PLUTO Data Dictionary, available online. An example is shown in Figure 4.1 where we have extracted the 'Commercial and Office Buildings' land use category for the whole of New York City and displayed it as a small 3D model. If we are familiar with the city it may confirm what we already knew, but it gives precise attributional and spatial information in relation to land use in New York City and, in a GIS setting, we can query individual parcels and obtain full details on each plot.

The MapPLUTO example helps demonstrate that the basic view of 'data' as raw, unstructured numbers does not sit well with what we tend to think of as 'data' in a GIS sense. It can cause some confusion, but so long as we are aware of the different definitions it should not in practice make any difference to our work. Regardless of whether our starting point is data or information, however, we need to understand the purpose of analysis and what the ultimate objectives of our work should be. In the built environment, this will differ from

Figure 4.1 *New York City land use data (MapPLUTO)*

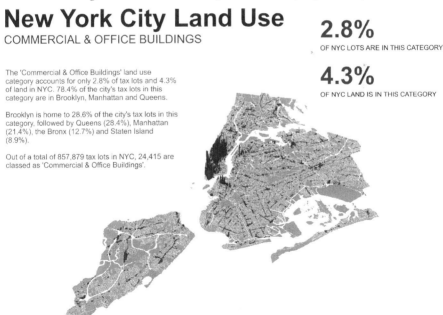

case to case, but it is often aimed at the creation of new knowledge and used as the basis for decision making, which, in other terms might be thought of as 'wisdom'. The next section explores this progression more closely.

DIKW: does data always lead to wisdom? (clue: no!)

When working in a GIS environment there are a number of possible goals. One might simply be exploratory, a kind of 'let's see what we have got' approach. Most users will be familiar with this workflow when they load a new dataset into their GIS and explore it for the first time. It can be quite exciting and the data itself can help us generate new questions that we might otherwise never have considered.

Another goal might be analytical, perhaps focusing on deriving some kind of spatial statistics from existing data. Alternatively, we may just begin with an overarching research question, such as 'where should we build this Taco Bell if we want it to be accessible by the largest number of people?'. There are many more possible use cases in GIS, but in the world of planning and the built environment GIS is very often used for location-based decision support. In this sense, it is useful to think about the progression from data to wisdom – and the steps in between – because it can help us to develop an appropriate workflow and also help guide our analytical objectives.

Although we think there is an important relationship between data, information, knowledge and wisdom in the world of GIS, we also need to make some important points before proceeding any further.

- Whereas in the world of information science data may refer to a raw, unstructured, uncontextualised form, in the world of geographic information science it typically refers, strictly speaking, to 'geo-information'. It is useful to make the distinction because it serves as a reminder that when we are working with spatial datasets such as Shapefiles the underlying data has already been given structure and meaning.
- We do not think that the relationship between data, information, knowledge and wisdom is necessarily a linear one. In fact, it is entirely possible that someone who commissions a piece of GIS analysis already knows what they want to do and simply needs some suitable empirical work to provide seemingly rigorous justification to decisions already taken.
- The 'wisdom' part of this framework relies not on technical skill but on carefully considered analytical judgement. The question of whether someone has made a 'wise' decision is a subjective one and relates to our basic view of how the world 'should be'. This is what we call a 'normative' question and it is important here to remember that GIS analysis will never have all the answers. The most important piece of hardware is our brain and we must be very careful to use it at all times and not become subservient to any analytical processes we employ, however sophisticated and exciting they may be.

- Most typically, GIS analysis in planning and the built environment will aim to provide clear information or generate knowledge as a basis for decision making. Fundamental questions about what can be known (ontology) and how we can know it (epistemology) therefore underlie our methodological approaches, even if we do not know it.

Before moving on, we'll now provide a small worked example of one possible route from data to wisdom using a hypothetical example from the natural world.

In the Highlands of Scotland, the small biting insect known as the 'midge' or 'midgie' often ruins people's experience of the outdoors. It has been reported at densities of up to 20 million per hectare and anyone familiar with walking or camping in the Highlands will have no trouble believing this. If we were planning a mountain camping expedition during summer (peak season for the midge) it would be extremely *wise* to plan ahead and make some attempt to minimise the risk of exposure. Put simply, wisdom would dictate that we should pitch our tent in the 'least bad' location. But where would this be? Well, this is where GIS-based spatial analysis comes in handy.

In advance of our trip, we have generated a list of x and y coordinates at a density which mirrors the spatial distribution of the midge based on underlying land classification values. This list of coordinate pair numbers are our *data*, but they constitute *information* in this context as we know they represent a simulated midge density coverage. This point distribution layer was generated for a particular area of the Cairngorm Mountains (see Figure 4.2) because that is where we want to pitch our tent. Luckily for us, we have some extra knowledge here. We know that in more windy, exposed areas we are less likely to be affected by midge swarms and that these areas are likely to be at higher elevations. We also know that individual midges have a fairly limited range. Thanks to Ordnance Survey, the national mapping agency of Great Britain, we have a raster layer containing detailed elevation data which we can then use to support our location-based decision making.

In this hypothetical example, we derive new information by using standard GIS tools. First, we generate a new raster layer which provides a summary of the density of midges within a 500 m radius. Then we use this new layer, in combination with the Ordnance Survey elevation layer, to perform a raster calculation to identify all areas with a density of less than 1000 per hectare and elevation above 750 m. Our options would be limited, but if we print this map and take it with us it will give us additional useful knowledge and we ought to be able to minimise the impact of the notorious Highland midge. The resulting map of final potential campsite locations (as 250 × 250 m cells) is shown in Figure 4.2.

This kind of example can be applied to all kinds of spatial decision-making scenarios (see also Chapter Nine), but ultimately the final decision on what one 'should' do comes down to personal judgement and, very often in the context of planning and the built environment, political and economic considerations. However, if our data is accurate and our methods robust then the knowledge we

Figure 4.2   *Suitable campsite areas based on multi-criteria analysis*

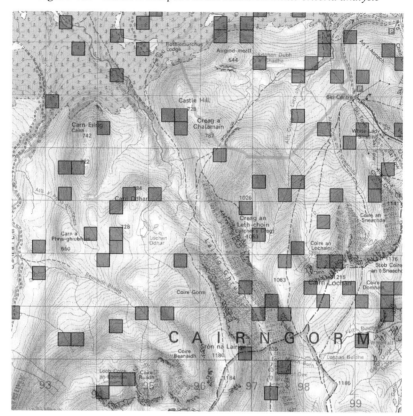

base our decisions on is more likely to be valid, but they will rarely be perfect. This brings to mind the famous quote from the statistician George E. P. Box who said that 'all models are wrong, but some are useful'. GIS can never give us wisdom, but it can give us the knowledge we need to make wise decisions, and so long as we do not think GIS alone can solve our problems we are on the right track.

Data models, file formats and image formats

The wider GIS literature does a very good job of explaining the basic differences between the two major data models in geographic information science, so we will only briefly recap on them here, before going into more detail on data types and formats. The key thing to remember here is that a 'model' is a simplified representation of the world and, as such, data based on either the vector or the raster models is always approximations of the real world rather than exact replications of it.

On the one hand, we have vector data or, more accurately, the vector data model. The best way to think about vector data is by thinking about polygons, lines or points defined by a series of coordinates. For example, a point layer will normally be defined by a series of unique x and y coordinates, a line layer will be defined by a set of linked x and y coordinates and a polygon will be defined by a series of x and y coordinates that begin and end in the same place (to close the polygon). The three basic geometry types of points, lines and polygons are one of the defining features of data handling in many GIS software packages, including ArcGIS, MapInfo and QGIS. These software packages read a vector data file format and translate coordinate information to spatial objects that appear on screen.

The vector data model in GIS represents things in the real world as points, lines and polygons and is quite efficient in terms of the space it takes up on our hard drives. The most commonly used vector data format is ESRI's Shapefile, but there are many others, as we explain later, in the section below on GIS file formats.

The other main data type we will encounter in GIS is raster data or, more accurately, the raster data model. Instead of displaying spatial objects as a series of points, lines or polygons, raster data uses cells (normally square) to represent features on the earth. An example of this would be global elevation data produced by NASA as part of its Shuttle Radar Topography Mission. This dataset comprises a set of individual raster tiles covering most of the land surface of the earth, at a spatial resolution of 90 m. Each 90 m cell has an elevation value associated with it and each individually downloaded tile is 6000 × 6000 pixels in size (or about 540 km).

One interesting thing about these different data types that is not always communicated to GIS students is that raster model applies to many common image formats we all know and use on a regular basis. Vector and raster are by no means unique to GIS. For example, the JPG images you create when you take a photo are a type of compressed raster and many graphics we see in PDF documents are in vector format. One simple way to tell the difference is to zoom in several times. If an image becomes fuzzy it is almost certainly a raster file format and if it remains crisp and clear it is almost certainly vector.

Another common aspect of these formats we sometimes overlook is that when working with GIS data in the context of urban planning and the built environment we often work with vector data (e.g. ESRI Shapefiles) and export our final map to a raster format (such as PNG) for final display in reports, presentations or posters. Most of the time we do not need to worry about the distinction between the raster and vector data models because it has already been predetermined by the data provider, but if the need arises we can convert from raster to vector, or vice versa, in many common desktop GIS programmes.

The topics of file formats and image formats may not be the most stimulating of subjects, but understanding them is critical to successful analysis and presentation in GIS so the next part of this section goes into more detail on the most important major file and image formats you will encounter when undertaking analysis of the urban environment. The obvious starting point for this is ESRI's well-known Shapefile format, as described in Box 4.2.

Box 4.2   The mighty Shapefile

The longevity of the ESRI Shapefile format is testament to the fact that it simply works for most GIS users. However, the term 'Shapefile' itself is a bit of a misnomer that sometimes causes problems for less experienced users who think of it as a single file when in fact it is a collection of at least three. This is set out clearly in ESRI's (1998) *Shapefile Technical Description* document. The basic description of the file format is that the 'geometry for a feature is stored as a shape comprising a set of vector coordinates', in a file with a .shp extension (ESRI refers to this as the 'main file'). This *always* needs to be accompanied by an Index file (the .shx file part) and a dBase table (the .DBF part) which stores the attribute data associated with spatial features. The dBase part of a Shapefile can be opened in most common spreadsheet packages (such as Excel and LibreOffice), but if it is part of a Shapefile it is wise not to edit it in this way. Many GIS instructors will recall the confusion of new students who try to load a Shapefile after downloading only the .shp part but see nothing on screen when they load it into a GIS. Additionally, a Shapefile can have a .prj part, which defines the projection. This is just a text file in the 'well-known text' format. You can see this for yourself if you open a .prj file in a text editor. Despite its longevity, however, the Shapefile has many critics and ESRI itself often encourages analysts to use an alternative data structure known as the file geodatabase, which is more efficient and flexible. More recently, the emergence of the GeoJSON format in web mapping applications has led a new cohort of users to question the viability of the Shapefile. Nonetheless, it has served the GIS community well and we think it will remain an important spatial file format for years to come.

GIS file formats

Understanding file formats is critically important in the world of GIS. Most people only work with a few different file formats, but experienced GIS analysts should be familiar with as many as possible. The Shapefile might be the most widely known, but you should definitely be able to tell the difference between your KML, your DXF and your TAB formats. Therefore, the rest of this subsection briefly explains a variety of the most common and important GIS file formats. For a comprehensive listing, check the GDAL vector formats list online (<https://www.gdal.org/ogr_formats.html>) or the equivalent listing for raster formats.

Common vector data formats

SHP – as explained in Box 4.2, ESRI's Shapefile format is very widely known and used in the GIS industry and is the mainstay of much GIS analysis. It has been challenged by other file formats over the years but remains the default spatial data format for many users.

GPKG – the GeoPackage is the new kid on the block, so to speak. Unlike the Shapefile format, it is an open, non-proprietary, platform-independent and standards-based geospatial data format. What this means in simple terms is that it is very flexible and adaptable. If any geospatial format is to challenge the Shapefile's dominance, this is it. It is actually a kind of spatial data container and supports both vector and raster formats, but we list it here because of its likely impact because we think future vector data publishers are most likely to adopt it.

TAB – the MapInfo TAB file format is, as the name suggests, mainly used by MapInfo users. It is sometimes referred to as the 'MapInfo native format' as well, and like ESRI's Shapefile format it is a proprietary format. As with the Shapefile format, the TAB format requires additional files in order to display geographic information. What this typically means in practice is that users of this format will see files with the following extensions in their working folder when using the TAB format: .DAT, .ID, .MAP, .IND.

KML – this file acronym stands for Keyhole Markup Language and was originally developed for use within Google Earth but has now become more widely used in web mapping applications. For non-GIS users, this file format might be their first encounter with a spatial dataset.

GML – this stands for Geography Markup Language and, like KML, it displays vector features in a GIS. It was developed by the Open Geographic Consortium in 2000.

DXF – this refers to Drawing Exchange Format and is a computer-aided design format used in applications such as Autodesk's AutoCAD software. The point of this 'exchange' format is that it allows data used in design software to be imported into a GIS. This is particularly useful in built environment disciplines where different professionals tend to favour certain tools and do not necessarily use GIS.

DWG – this is another file format native to computer-aided design packages and, like DXF, can be imported and manipulated in desktop GIS software. This is particularly useful if, for example, urban designers using AutoDesk are working with urban planners who use ArcGIS.

GeoJSON – this is an open standard file format for storing simple geographic features. The format was launched in 2008 and is now widely used in web mapping applications such as CartoDB and Leaflet.

TopoJSON – this close relative of GeoJSON includes information on topology (information on the relationships between individual features) and typically results in smaller file sizes than GeoJSON.

Common raster data formats

GeoTIFF – this is a geographical variant of the common Tagged Image File Format (TIFF). One important difference between a TIFF and a GeoTIFF is that the latter includes georeferencing information so that a GIS can position the data correctly. A standard, non-geographic TIFF file can also be georeferenced within a GIS so long as it is accompanied in the same folder by a

.TFW file, also known as a 'world file'. The world file, put simply, tells the GIS where the TIFF file should be located.

ESRI Grid – this raster file format comes in two types. One is the proprietary format, known as the Arc GRID, and the other is non-proprietary and known as ASCII GRID. In the latter, ASCII stands for the American Standard Code for Information Interchange (see the section 'The importance of structured data' in Chapter 3), which is a type of character-encoding used in computing. Like all raster formats, both types of this format are based on cells which each have an attribute assigned to them. The file format can store decimal numbers or integers.

ADRG – this raster file format is used by the US military and the National Geospatial-Intelligence Agency (NGA). ADRG stands for 'Arc Digitized Raster Graphic' and is a standard NIMA format, designed in the late 1980s for raster map display.

JPEG2000 – this is an open source raster format, not widely used in mainstream GIS but important nonetheless. It is related to the original JPEG format but includes georeferencing capabilities. JP2 files (as they are known) can be added to your GIS and correctly located on the surface of the earth in the same way as GeoTIFF images.

Other raster formats – there are fewer widely used raster image formats in the world of GIS for planning and the built environment, but other formats users may come across are the ERDAS IMG format, MrSID, ECW and RPF. The greatest likelihood is that you would be using the first two formats listed above in any GIS work since these formats are by far the most widely used in proprietary and open source GIS applications in our fields. As we note in the list of data formats above, it is important to recognise the flexibility of the GeoPackage format and the fact that it can also contain raster data.

Other GIS data formats

Observant readers will have noticed that, so far, we have not mentioned the third dimension. This is important, since 3D GIS applications are increasingly common and particularly so in the built environment. Software like ESRI's CityEngine has begun to revolutionise our 3D modelling capabilities so it is important to be aware of other formats which do not necessarily fit so neatly into the raster/vector typology. One obvious example widely used in landscape mapping is ESRI's TIN format. A TIN is a triangulated irregular network and this file format can be used in applications such as ESRI's ArcScene to render 3D models of geographical features.

GIS users in the United States may be particularly familiar with the Digital Elevation Model (DEM) format used by the US Geological Survey (USGS). This raster-based geospatial data format was developed by the USGS for displaying elevation in the United States but is also used throughout the world. There are several other less well-known GIS data formats but we have only covered the main ones here. The next section looks at the file formats we *export*, rather than *import*, from a GIS.

Important image formats in GIS

We have discussed the main file formats you will come across when working with data in a GIS but it is also important to think about the file formats you will need to be familiar with when saving and exporting maps from your GIS projects. After all, there is no point producing a beautiful piece of spatial data analysis if it is then shared in a low-resolution, lossy file format which other users cannot make the most of. This is particularly true in built environment applications where accurate and high-quality model, map and plan reproduction can be critical to securing support for projects. Experienced GIS users will be familiar with the following scenario. You have conducted robust, rigorous analysis, spent hours making sure a map looks beautiful before saving it to a high-quality image format. You then hand it over to another person, who perhaps is using the image in a report, and they resize your map and make further edits to it before eventually turning it into a fuzzy, pixelated image in a PDF. We cannot necessarily control this, but if we understand how image formats work we can minimise the risk. Understanding the image formats below is a good first step.

In most GIS software packages, there are a few ways to export maps, but we always recommend saving maps at an appropriate image resolution (dpi) and using a format which best fits the end use. Depending on what your map is to be used for, a 300 dpi PNG or a 600 dpi TIF may be suitable, but in nearly every case accepting the default (e.g. 96 dpi JPG) is not a good idea. Thankfully, modern GIS software provides lots of flexibility in this regard, and tools such as QGIS, ArcGIS and MapInfo allow us to choose from a wide variety of image formats and resolutions. The list below explains the different formats but first we explain a little bit more about 'dpi'.

Box 4.3   Dots per inch (dpi or DPI)

DPI stands for 'dots per inch' so readers more familiar with the metric system might find this measure a little archaic. Nonetheless, it is the standard measure of dot density in printing and, in any case, 'dots per 2.54 cm' is not very catchy. Pixels per inch (PPI) is the equivalent measure for on-screen resolution, or pixel density. DPI is a 2D measure, so it is the number of dots that fit into a linear inch on a page. The higher the number, the higher quality the final image will be. Some GIS packages used to begin with a default DPI of 96, which is okay for on-screen viewing but not suitable for print. Therefore, GIS users should generally opt for a much higher DPI in their work and especially so if it is to be printed (at least 300 dpi is a good rule of thumb here). Ultimately, it is the

$\rightarrow$

→

intended end use that should help you decide what DPI to save at. The question then might reasonably be 'how big is a dot'? This is determined by your printer. For a printer capable of printing at 600 dpi, or 600 dots per 2.54 cm, each dot would be 1/600th of an inch at the maximum resolution – that is, 0.0423 mm for each dot. In general, we would always recommend a DPI of 300 or more so that you can view on screen and print at a good quality. How high can you take DPI? This depends on your computer system's memory so try setting DPI to 1600 and see what happens – if it works, the file size will be gigantic and the actual size of the image on screen will also be very large.

JPG – we start with this raster file format because it is so widely known and most of us will see or capture images in this format every day. JPG is a contraction of JPEG, which stands for Joint Photographic Experts Group so the clue is in the name; this image format is good for photographs but it performs poorly in map reproduction because it is a 'lossy' format. This means that the original quality of the image is reduced through a compression algorithm. You will often notice blurring of colours near line boundaries in a JPG map export. We recommend not using this file format for exporting maps from your GIS project.

PNG – this is the file format we recommend for most on-screen and in-print uses (apart from professional publishing, where EPS or TIF is preferred). The Portable Network Graphics format uses lossless compression and as a consequence map exports in this format do not suffer from the problems seen in JPG exports. This file format was created as a non-proprietary replacement for the GIF image format, developed by CompuServe in 1987.

GIF – this file format has become synonymous with animations of cats and other Internet oddities, but of course can be used as an export format in most desktop GIS settings. Like PNG, GIF also supports lossless compression, which leads to high-quality images and relatively small file sizes.

TIF – also known as TIFF, the Tagged Image File Format is often requested by end users who want to edit images further or use them in print. File sizes for the TIF format are much larger than PNG, for example, so are normally best avoided for on-screen use and sharing between users over email. This format can be used without compression or with Lempel–Ziv–Welch compression (LZW). This sounds daunting but users only need to know that LZW compression is very efficient in reducing file size and this process is handled by your software.

PDF – most desktop GIS software will allow you to export maps to the Portable Document Format. This format is great for sharing across multiple platforms and for sharing documents on the Internet but is not good if you want your users to be able to reuse your mapping. In short, this format is best reserved for when an end user requests it or there is another good reason to use it.

EPS – this stands for Encapsulated PostScript format, and is a standard widely used in the publishing industry for high-quality graphics. It is not supported by all desktop GIS platforms but ESRI's ArcGIS allows user to export to EPS.

Other formats – the most commonly used formats are listed above, and these cover the majority of use cases in planning and built environment disciplines. Other formats users may wish to export to include AI (Adobe Illustrator – useful for further processing in Adobe software) and SVG (Scalable Vector Graphics – often used in web browsers). The older BMP (bitmap) format is still supported in desktop GIS but rarely used these days so we do not recommend exporting to this format. Other formats, such as Windows Enhanced Metafile (EMF) and ICO (for icons) can also be generated in a desktop GIS environment but most users will have no need for these formats.

Finally, it is useful to understand what kind of file sizes are associated with the most common image formats. For this purpose, we have mapped a small area of central London (see Figure 4.3) using very detailed building outline data from the Ordnance Survey. This was mapped in QGIS 2.10 with default export settings and saved at 150 dpi, 300 dpi, 600 dpi and 1200 dpi for the JPG, PNG and uncompressed TIF file formats. The resulting file sizes are shown in Table 4.1. Note that for the TIF format, every two-fold increase in dpi results in a four-fold increase in file size. For JPG and PNG, this scaling factor is between 2.3 and 3.3 so the increase in file size as dpi increases is not so dramatic.

Figure 4.3   *Buildings in Central London – from OS OpenData VectorMap Local*

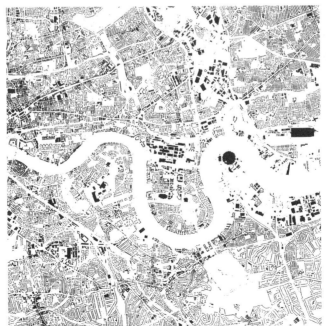

Table 4.1   *Comparison of file sizes of different file types and resolutions*

	File size (MB)		
DPI	*JPG*	*PNG*	*TIF*
150	0.7	2.5	8.5
300	2.4	7.0	34.0
600	3.6	16.8	136.0
1200	16.1	38.7	544.0

* Note that it is possible to change the export settings for different image formats – this is an illustrative example of default file sizes produced by different formats.

Contemporary data buzzwords: 'open' and 'big'

It would be remiss of us to write a chapter on data without mentioning two terms which have risen to prominence since the early 2010s. 'Open' data and 'big' data are often talked about as being the basis for a revolution in our understanding of the world and everything in it. Well, this is perhaps an exaggeration, but we think it is important for people working in the field of GIS to understand what they are and why they matter. We now deal with each of these in turn before moving on to the much more important topic of 'bad data'.

The term 'open data' has risen to prominence as governments across the world have sought – ostensibly at least – to increase transparency and accountability by releasing to the public vast swathes of previously hidden or expensive data. The definition provided by Open Knowledge International (2019) describes open data simply and clearly as:

> Open data is data that can be freely used, re-used and redistributed by anyone – subject only, at most, to the requirement to attribute and sharealike.

In the world of GIS, this represents something of a seismic shift, but of course the amount of open data varies by nation. Having said this, many nations now have extensive open data portals, such as data.gov in the United States, data. gov.uk in the United Kingdom and data.overheid.nl in the Netherlands. As of 2018 there were more than 2600 open data portals around the world.

Clearly, a lot of the open data now available is not geographic, but a good quantity is and there are in fact many dedicated open geodata portals. Excellent examples at the city level include the 'BYTES of the BIG APPLE' website from New York's Department of City Planning (http://www.nyc.gov/html/dcp/html/ bytes/applbyte.shtml) and Amsterdam's richly detailed open geodata portal (http://maps.amsterdam.nl/open_geodata/). At the national level, Great Britain's OS OpenData, launched in 2010, provides an immensely detailed set of GIS data resources for all of Great Britain; and with the addition of open GIS data for Northern Ireland, UK analysts now have complete national coverage of open data. In addition to official sources, OpenStreetMap data for all parts of the world, and in varying levels of detail, can now easily be obtained for use and analysis in GIS from organisations such as GEOFABRIK, which provide 'off-the-shelf' OSM data in ESRI Shapefile format (http://www.geofabrik.de/data/download.html). This volunteered geographic information is rapidly expanding and for many nations can now rival official sources for quality and coverage.

Open data and big data are not mutually exclusive terms, but the latter tends to refer to datasets that are so big they cannot easily be handled with standard desktop computing tools. They could also be open, but often they are not. Debate rages about the exact definition of big data, but for our purposes we define it within the GIS context in terms of any dataset that is too large to be handled by a single, powerful desktop computer using mainstream applications. In GIS terms, this would still be within the realm of the gigabyte but computer scientists and others may scoff at the triviality of such low volume since they may engage with data at the level of the petabyte (1 million gigabytes), using supercomputers and tools like Hadoop, an open source software framework for handling very large datasets across clusters of multiple computers. We understand such distinctions but do not dwell on them here since all disciplines will treat volume differently. The important point about big data and its disciples is that they claim it has the power to offer new insights across a wide range of activities, from health sciences and retailing to the way our cities are governed. The truth is probably more prosaic so we remain cautious about the possibilities of big data, but enthusiastic about its potential.

Ultimately, in the context of helping us move from the nuts and bolts of raw data towards the holy grail of wisdom, open data and big data can help, but they often present us with additional problems. As any GIS analyst knows, data is inherently 'messy' and often needs a significant amount of pre-processing, cleaning and checking. Put simply, the problem of 'bad data' will always be with us, even if it is open or big. The next part of the chapter therefore considers 'bad data' in more detail, and offers practical suggestions for how to overcome it.

'Bad data'

The volume of data available to analysts today is quite astonishing. For example, within minutes we can download and view data from NASA's Shuttle Radar Topography Mission and begin mapping the world in high resolution, or we could download Detroit's Motor City Mapping GIS database and analyse land use across the city's 380,000 land parcels. If we were so inclined, we could also download the City of Amsterdam's honeybees dataset and explore their patterns of activity. No matter what we do, though, we need to be sure our data are of sufficiently high quality to make our analysis meaningful. Otherwise, we are at risk of entering the domain of 'gi-go' analysis (garbage in, garbage out). Unfortunately, not all data providers are as careful as NASA, the City of Detroit or the City of Amsterdam. In some cases, our data can be incomplete, error strewn, inconsistent, of unknown origin, out of date or otherwise problematic. There are many possible terms for this, but here we refer to it using the shorthand term of 'bad data'. Some of the reasons that being aware of this is so important include:

- If our data is not correctly georeferenced and our map data is in the wrong place, any spatial analyses we perform could be meaningless or, potentially misleading. This can often happen when a dataset is supplied in one projection (e.g. WGS84) and used in a geoprocessing operation with a dataset in a different projection (e.g. British National Grid).
- If our data contains a column we wish to use as a basis for a join – so that we can import non-spatial datasets and map them – then we need to be sure it is in the right format. This is one of the biggest problems for novice and intermediate GIS users who are often flummoxed by leading spaces in area codes, superfluous spaces elsewhere and inconsistent spellings.
- We also often receive data in the 'wrong' format. An example here might include when we are given a large tabular dataset in PDF format, as was the case in 2013 when HSBC bank in the United Kingdom released 10,000 rows of mortgage lending data in this format. This kind of practice is all too common so knowing how to unlock this kind of data is an important skill for GIS analysts.

Box 4.4   When data goes bad: the case of the Scottish Index of Multiple Deprivation, 2009

Across the United Kingdom, patterns of deprivation are captured by a series of official deprivation indices. These serve multiple purposes, including informing local agencies which areas are most in need and which areas should be targeted by different policies. They now form a critical component of the national data infrastructure and can also help local people understand how their areas are viewed in a key government metric. One way this has been communicated is through the publication of web maps, as in the case of the Scottish Index of Multiple Deprivation from 2009. On these maps, Scotland is divided into 6505 small areas (called Data Zones), each with about 800 residents. In theory, this allows people to identify at a local level where their area ranks compared to all other areas. However, when this data was released in web map format in 2009, we immediately identified a problem. Owing to our unhealthy knowledge of the statistical geography of Scotland, we could see there was some misalignment between Data Zones and the underlying road network. The 'most deprived' Data Zone in Scotland at this time was home to Celtic Park, home of the world-famous Celtic Football Club, but the boundaries of the Data Zone were in the wrong place. This was checked in a GIS by one of the authors and the problem was communicated to the GIS team at the Scottish Government.

→

We identified that the problem arose because of a map projection error due to a mismatch between the British National Grid projection of the original data and the WGS84 projection of the web mapping platform. This resulted in a displacement of around 60 m for each Data Zone – a small distance, but large enough to place some areas in the wrong street. Thankfully, the error applied only to the web mapping platform but it is a good example of a case where data error could lead to someone drawing the wrong conclusions from seemingly accurate data. As you can see in the images below, the differences are subtle, yet they are very important.

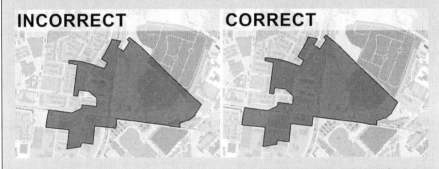

Note the way the incorrect image does not align with streets and intersections the way the correct one does. This kind of thing is sometimes a tell-tale sign of 'bad data'.

Bad data will never go away, so it is important to (1) be able to identify it when you see it and (2) know what to do to fix it, if this is even possible. The online news outlet Quartz maintains an excellent *Guide to Bad Data* on GitHub, which we highly recommend (<https://github.com/Quartz/bad-data-guide>). It covers common issues such as missing values and data formatting, as well as a whole lot more. Having a good knowledge of the kind of data problems you are likely to encounter (and being a good data wrangler) is not very glamorous but it is, we think, one of the most important skills for any spatial data analyst.

From data to wisdom? Not so fast!

At the start of this chapter we asked 'if data is the currency of GIS, how should we spend it?' The answer, in short, is 'wisely'. This brings us naturally to the issue of whether data is simply the first stepping stone on the way to wisdom. We hope we have demonstrated that we do not think this is the case and that, in the world of spatial data, we need a comprehensive understanding of what data is, how it relates to information and knowledge, and the two main data models. If we want our analyses to be presented and interpreted intelligibly, we should also have a firm grasp of file formats, image formats and know what to do when we inevitably encounter 'bad data'. If we have these skills and sufficient technical nous, then our spatial analyses can be powerful and effective, but they may never lead to wisdom since it is not itself within the domain of GIS and, anyway, we do not think the data–information–knowledge–wisdom relationship is a linear one. This should be clear to anyone working in fields related to urban planning and the built environment, where the idiosyncrasies of human activity, the unpredictability of urban life and the political and fiscal nature of decision making complicate our analyses. Any potential 'wisdom' we might hope to bestow on decision makers might get lost among the realities of urban planning, and any 'knowledge' we might hope to provide might be challenged on the basis of our understanding and handling of the underlying information. In this sense, then, we would do well to take heed of the words from T. S. Eliot's 'Choruses from the Rock' (1934) where he asks 'where is the wisdom we have lost in knowledge?, where is the knowledge we have lost in information?'. GIS *may* help us move along the road from data to wisdom, but the path is littered with obstacles and the destination may always remain just over the horizon. So long as we understand this, everything should be okay.

Chapter 5

Geovisualisation: Communicating with Spatial Data

Introduction

According to Longley and colleagues (2015), there are four main purposes of geovisualisation: exploration, synthesis, presentation and analysis. We concur with this assessment, particularly since we are writing for users of GIS in urban planning and the built environment, where such objectives are both necessary and worthwhile. But geovisualisation can also be used more superficially, and sometimes it can even be fun! Further, it can also serve as the spatial equivalent of what Darrell Huff called the 'gee-whiz graph', in *How to Lie with Statistics* (1954). The emergence in recent years of vast open datasets, and new tools to explore them with, has led to a proliferation of geovisualisations and, in turn, their visibility beyond the world of GIS. This chapter therefore focuses on the topic of geovisualisation from the perspective of communicating spatial data effectively within the domain of urban planning and the built environment.

In the next section, we focus on what geovisualisation is, and the question of whether it is just a fancy term for 'mapping'. We think not, but it bears further scrutiny. We also discuss recent advances in geovisualisation and explain why we think it is such an important part of geographic information science. Following this, we then explore the purpose of geovisualisation in more depth, building on the ideas of Longley and colleagues (2015) and others. Too often, excellent analyses are let down by poorly conceived visuals and lack of forethought in relation to how the end result will be displayed, so we focus here on highlighting the power of geovisualisation to change, inform, inspire and educate. The question of 'doing' geovisualisation is always easier when we have some guiding principles to build on, so we go on to introduce our four 'principles for the orderly loss of information', following Rae (2009). These principles build on the ideas of the economist Kenneth Boulding (1970), who stated that 'knowledge is always gained by the orderly loss of information, that is, by condensing and abstracting and indexing the great buzzing confusion of information that comes from the world around us' (p. 2). In the context of today's open and big data deluge, these words really ring true and in the world of geovisualisation in particular we need to find a way to filter out the noise.

Beyond the more abstract explanation of purposes and principles, we then provide some guidance on where we think readers ought to look for inspiration and best practice examples of geovisualisation. The bad examples certainly outweigh the good, but we think that pointing out some seminal work – and explaining why it is so powerful – is the best way to learn. Here, as is so often the case, we can mine a rich seam of prior knowledge. Given the focus in this book on the built environment, we then devote a short section of the chapter to visualising the third dimension since, as we all know, buildings are not flat! With the emergence of powerful 3D geovisualisation tools such as ESRI's ArcScene, SketchUp and ESRI's CityEngine in particular, the skilled spatial data analyst has a powerful toolset with which to work. We also identify some pitfalls here and recommend when it is, and is not, best to map in 3D. This is followed by a look at mapping 'pointless points' and the question of the 'clueless choropleth'. The penultimate section looks at the emerging domains of augmented reality (AR) and virtual reality (VR) within the world of GIS. This is an introductory text, so we do not go into detail here, but we think it is important for readers to understand the potential uses of AR and VR in a built environment context.

The growing availability of data and spatial analysis tools has been a very positive development in recent years. This, coupled with the rise in social media, means that more geovisualisations than ever before are being produced and consumed, often by non-specialists. We do not necessarily think this is a bad thing, but we do see a need to take stock of their impact. Also, we think there is value in re-examining some of the accepted cartographic principles and standards which GIS and cartography professionals hold dear, particularly in light of the growing volume of interactive web maps produced by non-specialists. We strongly believe in the democratisation of spatial data analysis and geovisualisation, and we welcome the growing user base, so here we outline some recommendations for those who are new to the topic in the context of urban planning and the built environment. We conclude the chapter by offering three important geovisualisation principles that we think sum it up.

Geovisualisation: just a fancy word for 'mapping'?

The first thing to understand about 'geovisualisation' is that it is closely related to, and often overlaps with, other types of visualisation. It is certainly not new, but the contemporary vogue for 'dataviz' means that in recent years it has had more exposure than ever before. Just as data visualisation and statistical graphics have a long history (e.g. Playfair, 1801) geovisualisation can find historical precedents in the work of people like French engineer Charles Joseph Minard and later in seminal work by Tobler (1987) and Dorling (1991). To the uninitiated, 'geovisualisation' might just seem like a fancy word for 'mapping', but we argue that it is much more than this since it can include – particularly in the built environment – animation, scenario-building, modelling, exploration and even VR. It certainly involves mapping, but the two terms are not equivalents.

Presenting data visually has been a mainstay of human communication for well over a thousand years, going back at least to the time of Claudius Ptolemy, the Greco-Egyptian geographer and polymath. His world map of around AD 150, and later replications by others, portrayed the known world based on coordinates in a way we still identify with. The ubiquity of maps today means that we often take for granted our ability to view the world visually and it is easy to overlook what was once a radical new way of seeing the world. The same applies to non-spatial data visualisation, in which William Playfair was a pioneer. His *Commercial and Political Atlas* (1786) and *Statistical Breviary* (1801) are landmark texts in the visualisation of numerical data, and while they may seem quaint today, their potency remains high. The fact that the line, bar, pie and area charts devised by Playfair are still so widely used is indicative of the power of visualisation. In fact, regular users of the charting tools in Microsoft Excel might not be aware that they are using charting methods developed by William Playfair more than two hundred years ago. The visual display of quantitative information, as in the title of Edward Tufte's famous text *The Visual Display of Quantitative Information*, is today a form of global currency in which ideas are shared and shaped. The focus here, however, is on geovisualisation in particular; so, before going any further, we provide a non-exhaustive list of some forms of geovisualisation in use today.

- **Traditional maps** – what we mean here is maps of any areas of the world, at any scale, which attempt to represent geographic areas accurately in terms of shape, area or a combination of the two. Examples here would include political maps of the countries of the world, choropleth maps of US states or EU regions showing variables such as GDP per capita, dot maps of crime at the city scale or transport maps showing geographically accurate routes such as road networks. Traditional maps are now often referred to as 'static maps'.
- **Cartograms** – these kinds of geovisualisations typically distort shapes of areas according to some underlying variable in order to emphasise the relative importance of an issue. An excellent example of this is Ben Hennig's Worldmapper work, which produces distorted-area cartograms of the nations of the world based on a wide variety of topics, such as population, income and disease. As the worldmapper.org website says, this is the 'world as you've never seen it before'.
- **Interactive web maps** – these kinds of online maps allow map users to zoom, pan, click and otherwise interact with a spatial representation of data in a web browser. Google maps would be a very basic example here, as would maps produced with tools such as CartoDB, but a particularly impressive example is the EarthWindMap, a near real-time global wind map on an interactive globe by Cameron Beccario which is updated every three hours. The functionality and beauty of this geovisualisation make it one of the very best of its kind.

- **Animated maps** – it is possible now to quite easily add in a temporal dimension and show how things change over time, and this can be done with animated maps. A good example here would be animations that show patterns of commuting at the city scale. The authors have experimented with these approaches in the past, focusing on commuting patterns in the Bay Area around San Francisco in California. These simple models of transportation to and from work are a simple but powerful way of demonstrating a more complex underlying phenomenon.

- **3D maps** – it can be very tempting to introduce the third dimension into our mapping, since it can look very impressive and exciting. For example, we could take a normal choropleth map of US counties and then extrude individual counties according to their population densities, or use the New York City MapPluto dataset to produce a 3D model of buildings in Manhattan. Sometimes, however, introducing the third dimension can cause visual occlusion and end up hiding more than it reveals. We like these kinds of geovisualisations but they are hard to do well. As a rule, it is better to use 3D approaches when users can interact with the map and zoom, spin and pan around rather than a single flat image such as a PNG file.

- **Topological maps** – not to be confused with *topographical* (which shows terrain), a topological map is one in which the connections between parts are portrayed accurately, independently of the size, scale or geographical accuracy of the map. This comes from the study of topology in mathematics and sounds confusing. A simpler way to explain this is to say that London's world-famous Tube Map is a topological map. The network's 270 stations are portrayed accurately in relation to their connections with one another, but not in relation to their real-world geography. You would soon find this out if you tried to use the Tube Map to find your way round London on the surface! Its inventor, Harry Beck, realised that when travellers are on the Tube the most important thing is knowing how to get from one station to the next and which stations interchange with which other ones. This is the real beauty of a topological map.

- **Dasymetric maps** – this kind of map has become increasingly popular in recent years as more data has become available with which to make them. A dasymetric map is one where 'attribute data that is organised by a large or arbitrary area unit is more accurately distributed within that unit by the overlay of geographic boundaries that exclude, restrict, or confine the attribute in question' (ESRI, 2015). In the urban setting, this might be where a standard population-related choropleth map is combined with building outline data so that only areas with buildings are coloured and represented on the map. This can be a particularly effective means of overcoming the problems associated with choropleth maps where large geographic areas with few people can dominate the map and, sometimes, give a misleading view of the distribution of a variable. A particularly effective example of dasymetric mapping can be found on University College London's DataShine platform, where the dasymetric approach has been applied very effectively by spatial data visualisation expert Oliver O'Brien.

These are just some of the most common types of geovisualisations in use today. The different types listed above are not all mutually exclusive and there can be overlap between different types (e.g. a 3D animated map) but these form the core of what you might call the geovisualisation canon in an urban setting. What these and any other kinds of spatial or non-spatial visualisations have in common is that they provide accessible visual summaries of some underlying phenomena and, when done effectively, can be extremely powerful. This was also the rationale behind William Playfair's (1801) early statistical graphics approach, since he said that 'making an appeal to the eye when proportion and magnitude are concerned, is the best and readiest method of conveying a distinct idea' (p. 4). The fact that some geovisualisations today may actually hurt your eyes is another matter. The key point here is that we can think of geovisualisation as an 'appeal to the eye'.

Clearly, then, geovisualisation is not just a fancy word for 'mapping', though some might argue it is an appropriate term for 'fancy mapping'. But this would be to trivialise geovisualisation and the work of geovisualisation pioneers such as Menno-Jan Kraak, Alan M. MacEachren, Mei-Po Kwan and Anthony C. Robinson. The work of MacEachren in particular has been instrumental in advancing our understanding of the cognitive processes through which maps work and how our brains interact with them. Thinking about the cognitive impact of geovisualisation provides the perfect segue to the next section of the chapter, which focuses on the purpose of geovisualisation, and we now turn to this topic in more detail.

The purpose of geovisualisation

We began this chapter by referring to Longley and colleagues' (2015) four purposes of geovisualisation, which they set out as exploration, synthesis, analysis and presentation. Here we want to reflect on these in the context of geovisualisation in urban planning and the built environment, with some relevant examples. To do this, we will present a very simplified scenario using an urban dataset. For this, we will use the example of the Manhattan layer of New York City's MapPLUTO geospatial dataset, which was released by New York's Department of City Planning in 2014, and approach it using Longley and colleagues' (2015) four purposes. But, first, it is useful to say more about the characteristics of the MapPLUTO dataset (Box 5.1). After this, we then take exploration, synthesis, presentation and analysis in turn, in order to demonstrate the value of geovisualisation in an urban data setting.

Exploration (what have we got and what does it look like?)

Exploration is an excellent place to start thinking about geovisualisation. In fact, it is the starting point for all kinds of analysis in geographic information science. When we have a new dataset basic questions such as 'what have

Box 5.1　What is MapPLUTO?

MapPLUTO is New York City's spatial tax lot level dataset. PLUTO stands for Primary Land Use Tax Lot Output and this exists separately from MapPLUTO. The latter combines PLUTO with the New York City Department of Finance's Digital Tax Map (DTM), clipped to the shoreline of the city. The data are updated regularly and the version used here is the March 2015–June 2015 version 15v1 release. There are more than 80 separate fields in the MapPLUTO dataset, including variables such as each parcel's address, land use category, floor area, number of floors, assessed value and Borough code. This information, and much more, is contained in the PLUTO Data Dictionary. The MapPLUTO™ dataset is released in the ESRI Shapefile format at the individual Borough level for Bronx, Brooklyn, Manhattan, Queens and Staten Island, whereas the non-spatial PLUTO dataset is available as a single CSV file for the whole city. The dataset was released, to much fanfare, in summer 2013 and has since been used as the basis for a wide range of impressive geovisualisation outputs. Put simply, then, MapPLUTO is a perfect example of the value of open data on the one hand and the potential of geovisualisation on the other.

we got here?' and 'what does it look like?' should underpin our approach. If we ask these questions at the outset – and follow up on them through thorough exploration – then we are more likely to truly understand what we are working with and the kind of different things we could do with it, identify errors or anomalies, and generally produce more meaningful analyses at a later stage. In the case of MapPLUTO, when we load the data into our GIS we see a layer of spatial data in the shape of Manhattan, subdivided into over 40,000 individual land parcels. We can immediately see some prominent features, such as Central Park, and the famous gridded street pattern emerges clearly here, too. Since Manhattan is an island, we can also identify the various piers and wharfs positioned around the edges of this Borough and, just to the south, we can see Governors Island, the largest of a group of three islands (Figure 5.1).

When we interact with the data by clicking on an individual area with the Identify Features tool in QGIS, we can see the wide range of attributes contained in the dataset. For example, we can identify that Central Park is in Council Area 6, has a zip code of 10065, and is in School District 3 and Police Precinct 22. Let's assume now that we wanted to understand more about land use in Manhattan. For this, we can use MapPLUTO's Land Use variable, of which there are 13 individual classes. Symbolising the data using this categorical variable produces the result shown in Figure 5.2, which instantly provides us with a more detailed assessment of how land use is distributed across the Borough. In Figure 5.2, we have zoomed in to Lower Manhattan so that we can see more detail. It is not possible to view all 13 categories clearly when

Figure 5.1   *Exploring MapPLUTO data*

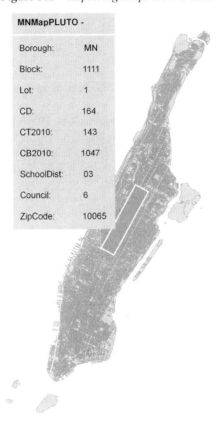

reproduced in greyscale so we have highlighted the location of Land Use category 5 (Commercial & Office Buildings).

We can continue to pan, zoom and explore the dataset spatially within the GIS environment from a spatial perspective, to build up a better understanding of the spatial structure of the data and any particularly important features. However, since we understand GIS from a database perspective, we also need to explore the underlying data via the attribute table, which can be done in all major desktop GIS packages. This allows us to identify high and low values, check for missing data, as well as spot things like spelling mistakes or errors in street names, and generally gives us a richer understanding of the data. It can be very tempting to dive straight into mapping, but this can result in flawed analysis and misleading presentation. Now that we have done the initial exploration, the next step is often synthesis. To take this further, we are going to look at the issue of the location of Manhattan's tallest buildings, which we can

Figure 5.2   *Commercial and office buildings in Lower Manhattan*

begin to understand via the 'NumFloors' variable in the MapPLUTO dataset. We combine this with another New York City GIS data layer in the section that follows.

Synthesis (can we see the wood for the trees?)

In this section, we will imagine that we need to understand more about the distribution of commercial and office buildings in Manhattan, in relation to their year of construction. In a GIS context, much of what would fall under the realm of 'synthesis' would be achieved through the analysis of multiple layers of data, but in the case of New York City's MapPLUTO, the underlying attribute table is so rich and full of value that the possibilities for meaningful synthesis are almost unlimited. If, as Longley and colleagues (2015) say, synthesis is about being able to see the wood for the trees, then it is absolutely essential in the case of this dataset, owing to the large number of small spatial units which are, essentially, lost in a forest of data.

To understand the geography of commercial and office buildings within Manhattan, we can simply filter the dataset using the Land Use field (05) and display this as a separate colour, as shown in Figure 5.3. In this example the 'synthesis' comes from combining location and attribute in relation to commercial and office buildings in Manhattan to provide a simple, at-a-glance overview of the spatial patterning of one land use class.

Figure 5.3   *Commercial and office buildings in Manhattan*

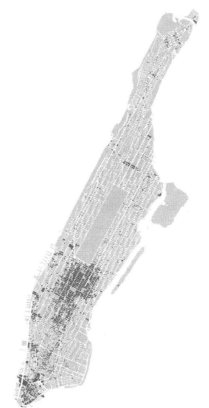

Analysis (what can it tell us?)

In this simplified example, we are going to imagine that, following the previous step, we now want to understand more about the distribution of commercial and office buildings along a single Manhattan avenue. In this case, we want to identify such buildings on Broadway, an avenue which runs along the length of Manhattan. This fits in with the true definition of analysis, which can be thought of as a detailed examination of the individual elements or structure of something. In this case, we are looking more closely at a single type of land use and its distribution along a very famous and important New York City thoroughfare. The result is shown in Figure 5.4.

Presentation (how can we display it?)

If we then want to communicate this information, rather than just explore and view it ourselves, then some careful thought about presentation is

Figure 5.4   *Commercial and office buildings along 'Broadway' in Manhattan*

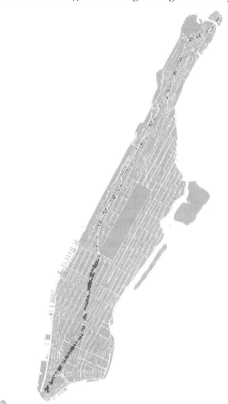

required. There are many factors we need to consider here, including the medium it will be viewed in (e.g. paper vs. online), the scale at which it will be viewed and the intended audience. In the Manhattan land use example, we are going to imagine that the intended audience are New York City architects and that they are particularly interested in the volume and size of these buildings along Broadway. We will therefore display the filtered data above in three dimensions, using the 'NumFloors' field in the MapPLUTO dataset in order to provide an approximation of building heights (Figure 5.5). The geovisualisation presented here is a static image, but in reality this information would be better presented in an interactive web browser format so that users can interact with the data, zoom, pan and view it from different perspectives.

This very stylised, simplified example demonstrates the inherent value of geovisualisation in an urban data setting since we began with a very large dataset of more than 40,000 individual polygons and then worked

Figure 5.5   *3D visualisation of commercial buildings on Broadway, Manhattan*

systematically to extract increasing levels of information from it. Through a geovisualisation approach, we were able to explore the data in considerable detail, synthesise different elements of it, analyse it further and then present a final geovisualisation focused on a specific topic. In reality, of course, geovisualisations in the real world are typically more complex, but they do not need to be. What *is* always sensible is to think of geovisualisation as a means of simplifying a more complex dataset with a view to communicating meaningful information to others. But to do this consistently well requires some fundamental principles to adhere to. For this purpose we now turn to four 'principles for the orderly loss of information' (Rae, 2009) which we think are a useful guide in GIS data management more generally but geovisualisation specifically.

'Principles for the orderly loss of information'

In previous years and decades, one of the biggest problems GIS analysts had was obtaining usable geographic data with which to work. Very often in the early days of GIS, the unavailability of spatial data made meaningful analyses impossible. Today, the situation is reversed and with the recent move to an open data culture in many nations, and the rise of 'big data' more generally, we need to be able to handle the data deluge and know how to deal with the sheer volume of data now in existence. This is where we invoke Rae's four 'principles for the orderly loss of information', drawing on Kenneth Boulding's (1970) famous dictum which stated that 'it is a very fundamental principle indeed that knowledge is always gained by the orderly loss of information, that is, by condensing and abstracting and indexing the great buzzing confusion of information that comes from the world around us into a form which we can appreciate and comprehend' (p. 2). We now present these principles here in written form, with reference to the MapPLUTO data introduced in this section.

Expansive inclusion – the first principle relates to always starting off with every possible data element at the outset, in addition to any related data that may add value. This allows us a greater degree of selectivity when decisions are being made about what to display and also facilitates improved query capability; though it will of course make geocomputation more demanding. In the case of mapping a large migration matrix, this is certainly the case. Any loss of information in geovisualisation should be as a result of analytical decision making and not by omission at the outset. In the context of the MapPLUTO dataset for Manhattan, this might simply involve working with the complete New York City MapPLUTO dataset at the outset in order to understand the data within the context of the other four Boroughs, but equally it might involve us incorporating other New York City datasets available from the same source. Working with a complete dataset at the beginning may also make error detection easier and reduce any time wasted at a later stage. There are obvious linkages here, therefore, with the geovisualisation purpose of exploration.

Iterative loss – the second principle that we can apply is one of iterative loss, so that the key trends and spatial structures within a dataset can be identified via a series of repetitive experiments whereby the data displayed is iteratively reduced. In the case of MapPLUTO and New York City, this may involve opting not to display larger polygons, such as Central Park, in order to draw attention to the more important locations of a particular land use class. In such a process, then, there is an inevitable balance to be struck between information and omission and, in a sense, this correlates quite closely with the geovisualisation principle of synthesis.

Simplicity from complexity – a third general guiding principle of geovisualisation is related to the skill of the analyst and can be defined as the need to derive simplicity from complexity. This is a fundamental skill in data analysis more generally, but is particularly important with large spatial datasets such as MapPLUTO where the volume of data, and its level of detail, has the potential to overwhelm. The level of difficulty here is very closely related to the overall size and complexity of the dataset, but in an era of data-rich GIS this is a significant challenge and one that must be taken seriously if we want our analyses to have explanatory value. In the context of New York City and individual tax lots, this may be something as simple as choosing to display only those buildings above a certain number of floors, or those in a particular land use class. Our view is that simplicity does not have to be simplistic and that the most powerful analyses in geovisualisation are in fact conceptually very simple. This principle therefore relates most obviously to the domain of analysis in geovisualisation more broadly.

Optimal compromise – finally, we can think of all the above under the rubric of optimal compromise, since we are simultaneously trying to optimise the effectiveness of display while making compromises in relation to what is either included or omitted. In each of the geovisualisations presented above, these principles have been applied, albeit in a very simple manner. From a geovisualisation point of view, optimal compromise is a recognition that we simply cannot do everything at once. In the context of MapPLUTO, this may mean not attempting to display all 11 of the city's land use classes in a single map, or it may mean only displaying data for a single street or district. In relation to Longley and colleagues' (2015) purposes of geovisualisation, therefore, this relates most closely to the presentation element, but, equally, it may relate more generally to the idea of projecting a 3D world on a flat piece of paper or computer screen.

We think that the best and most effective geovisualisations are, knowingly or not, based on the four principles outlined above, but, of course, they can easily be violated. In such instances, the end product is likely to be a less effective geovisualisation and, in the words of William Playfair, less likely to make 'an appeal to the eye'. More importantly, they are less likely to make a cognitive connection with the viewer and this has the potential to reduce comprehension and, ultimately, influence the end user. In the world of urban planning and the built environment, where understanding space and location are essential, this could be a significant problem. But, of course, this sounds quite negative so in the next section we offer a variety of source for inspiration in the world of geovisualisation.

Where to look for inspiration

In the world of visualisation more generally, the Internet is a great place to start for *bad* examples of the practice. Websites like WTF Visualizations and Junk Charts provide many egregious examples of bad practice. Similarly, in the world of GIS and cartography, Kenneth Field's 'Cartonerd' blog has many examples of less than stellar work from the geovisualisation world and further afield. While we acknowledge the importance of understanding bad practice, and how to avoid it, here, instead, we wish to offer more constructive advice on where one might look for inspiration in relation to geovisualisation examples for GIS analysts working in the fields of urban planning and the built environment more generally. Our view is that one should always have a working knowledge of 'best practice' in any field and understand what a good geovisualisation looks like and what makes it 'good'.

The problem here, of course, is that there is just so much stuff! With the increasing volume of data we have seen an exponential growth in the number of visual outputs published (mostly online) and many of these have been produced by people without a background in GIS or cartography. Some are beautiful and interesting, but many are not. This is a starting point for further investigation, and we divide our recommended inspirations into 'global mapping examples', 'open source pioneers' and 'styling and design'. We have chosen a limited selection here in order to avoid overwhelming the reader.

Global mapping examples

Many of us, when undertaking GIS work, focus on the neighbourhood or city scale. Still others focus on the national scale. But, of course, many issues that neighbourhoods, cities and countries face are in fact global challenges. It is in this context which we present some examples of best practice in relation to global mapping:

Worldmapper – billed as 'the world as you've never seen it before', the Worldmapper website is a collection of nearly 700 world maps, resized according to the subject of interest. The website was the brainchild of geovisualisation pioneers Ben Hennig and Danny Dorling of the University of Oxford in the United Kingdom.

NASA Earth Observatory – NASA in the United States has an unparalleled volume of global data, and makes excellent use of it on this Global Maps site. Described as a 'global view of what's happening on our planet', there is data on topics such as land surface temperature, fire outbreaks, total rainfall, vegetation and sea surface temperature anomaly. The site also includes many animations and links to the underlying data sources.

EarthWindMap – Cameron Beccario's beautiful, informative and functional global weather and environmental data globe is part work of art, part scientific exemplar. When the site loads, viewers see a live, animated global wind map projected onto an interactive spherical map in the web browser. But words alone do not do this justice so you should take a look yourself.

OpenStreetMap – it would be remiss of us not to mention OpenStreetMap here. We have already mentioned that the data is available to download but this inspirational collaborative project to create an editable map of the world also has an interactive global map online. Users can quickly see which parts of the world have not been mapped and begin to contribute data to the project. After more than a decade, OpenStreetMap now has more than two million users and frequently provides humanitarian aid in the form of geospatial intelligence in major global disasters, such as the 2010 Haiti earthquake.

Free and open source geospatial pioneers

The 2010s have been exciting times in the world of geovisualisation and GIS, with the growth in open source geospatial technology such as QGIS and OpenLayers and the growing contribution from those with a computer science and programming background. There are so many pioneers doing so many exciting things, but here we list some particularly prominent ones who we think readers ought to know about and follow up on. Featuring most prominently here are several leading QGIS developers:

Anita Graser – a self-described 'scientist, open source GIS advocate and data geovisualisation geek' based at the Austrian Institute of Technology in Vienna, Graser is a member of the QGIS Project Steering Committee and author of *Learning QGIS* (now in its second edition). Her 'Free and Open Source GIS Ramblings' blog is one of a small number of 'must-reads' in the field of open source GIS and she has been a key contributor to the development of geovisualisation techniques in open source GIS, and more widely.

Nyall Dawson – another leading figure on the development and use of QGIS, Dawson is a Melbourne, Australia based mapping, GIS, QGIS and MapBasic expert whose blog regularly provides technical instruction and cartographic inspiration.

Nathan Woodrow – a passionate advocate of open source GIS, Woodrow is an Australian technical consultant and GIS specialist for Digital Mapping Solutions. His regular contributions to the QGIS project and technical explanations on his blog are an invaluable source of knowledge for any aspiring GIS analyst.

Jason Davies – Davies is actually a freelance software engineer focused on the visualisation of challenging dataset and not an open source GIS user per se. However, one look at www.jasondavies.com and his work with spatial data in the d3 JavaScript library tells you why we included him here. His web pages are full of inspiring maps and graphics and he is a real master of visualising through code.

Mike Bostock – the originator of the d3 JavaScript library, Bostock was previously the graphics editor of the *New York Times*, a media outlet who are still pioneers in the field of interactive visualisation. Much of this was driven by Bostock. On his various web offerings, you'll see some stunning geovisualisations, including highly detailed maps from the US Midterm Elections, tutorials on mapping in d3 and cartograms on global manufacturing.

Styling and design

Knowing how to handle and map data is an extremely important skill in the world of GIS. But not knowing how to apply design and styling principles to your geovisualisation outputs can undermine your good work. Many a map was ruined by a poor colour scheme or ill-advised font, so that is why we include some key information sources under this category.

ColorBrewer – the first and most obvious place to start here is Cynthia Brewer's ColorBewer site. Billed as 'Color Advice for Maps', that is exactly what it is and it is an invaluable resource for the GIS world. It is based on rigorous academic research and can help you pick colour schemes which are colour-blind safe, print friendly or photocopy safe. You can select from multi-hue or single-hue schemes and sequential, diverging or qualitative data. In short, it is a 'must-read'.

Gretchen Peterson – a Colorado-based cartographer, Peterson's work has served as an inspiration to thousands of GIS professionals, cartographers, students and anyone with an interest in communicating clearly with geographic data. Her regularly updated blog is a great source of inspiration and news, and her *Cartographer's Toolkit: Colors, Typography, Patterns* and *GIS Cartography: A Guide to Effective Map Design* books are key publications in the field, highly accessible and eminently readable.

Atlas of Design – this gallery of beautiful and inspiring maps from across the world is now in two volumes, with a third in progress. It includes work by geovisualisation experts such as Eric Fischer, Roger Smith, Daniel P. Huffman, Andrea Hansen, Eleanor Lutz, Andy Woodruff and John Nelson.

Axis Maps – the Cartography Guide from Axis Maps is the final, but most important, resource we will list here. The authors very humbly say that they want to 'share some insights and tips for making thematic maps' but in reality this is a treasure trove of good advice for GIS cartography for all levels of user. Axis Maps is led by Andy Woodruff on the development side and by Ben Sheeshly on design and is based in Hewitt, Texas. The guide was originally written for indiemapper.com in 2010 but has been very thoughtfully brought together in one place for all to use.

Other sources of inspiration

It can be difficult to know where to turn for inspiration in the field of geovisualisation these days, such is the dizzying array of blogs, tweets and messages with a geographic focus. We offer the above very much as a starting point, but we also recommend spending some time looking at the work of the following individuals or institutions, all of which are easy to find online through your favourite search engine: Edward Tufte, the UX Blog from IDV Solutions, the QGIS Map Showcase on Flickr, Alberto Cairo (University of Miami), Joshua Stevens (NASA), Anna Powell-Smith (Flourish Studio), the *Financial Times* and *Washington Post*'s graphics pages, CartoDB, MapBox and the GeoDa Center at Arizona State University. Spending some time online looking at these resources and individuals will help you get a sense of what works when it comes to geovisualisation and help you improve your own practice. Before concluding this chapter, we now turn to two final topics which are particularly important in the world of urban planning and the built environment. The first is the question of the third dimension and the second is the thornier issue of point mapping and problematic choropleths.

Visualising the third dimension

As stated in the introduction, the use of 3D mapping can be particularly effective in built environment disciplines so we examine this issue here. Before going any further, however, we should say that much of what might appear to be 3D in the world of GIS is more properly referred to as 2.5D, since they are not 'true' 3D representations, but we will not dwell on that here. Instead, we want to say a little more about the use of the vertical dimension, or z value, in geovisualisation. This is one area in which ESRI software such as ArcScene, and now CityEngine, is invaluable. Here we identify three possible use cases for mapping using the third dimension, with examples for each.

Mapping building polygons

Detailed building outline data is available for many cities across the world via OpenStreetMap. In Great Britain, we now have highly detailed building outline polygons available as open data, and this has greatly expanded the potential user base for mapping urban environments in three dimensions. This can be a particularly effective way of modelling cities, but there are two points that need to be kept in mind when doing so. First, if we wish our representations to be accurate, we need to obtain accurate building height data and overlay this on an accurate terrain model. Second, we need to be very aware of the potential for visual occlusion caused by the varying heights of buildings. Put simply, there is no point producing 3D mapping if the introduction of a z factor merely serves as a visual impediment to seeing some important features. This is a particular problem in cities with many tall buildings, as in the case of San Francisco (Figure 5.6).

Choropleth maps

There are many problems with choropleth maps (see the next section for an example) but in some cases the introduction of the third dimension can provide additional useful information. Our view is that most of the time mapping in 3D is best avoided for choropleths, but there are cases when it can add another dimension of useful information, particularly in relation to highlighting anomalies. For example, one of the problems with the traditional choropleth is within-class variation. So, if we wanted to map daytime population density across counties in the lower 48 states of the United States, there would inevitably be

Figure 5.6   *Extruded building polygons in San Francisco, California*

a large bias towards major urban centres such as New York, Chicago and Los Angeles. Consequently, the numerical breaks between choropleth classes would have to be very carefully chosen. Even so, the variation in values within classes is likely to be high, so the massive peaks in daytime population density are unlikely to be picked up, and certainly not emphasised, in cities such as San Francisco, Denver, Washington, Boston and – most obviously – New York City. This can be seen in the stylised geovisualisation in Figure 5.7, where we have

Figure 5.7   *An extruded choropleth map of US population density*

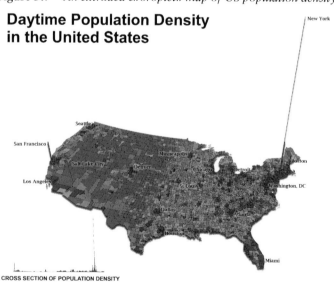

mapped daytime population density across the Lower 48 states in choropleth format, and then extruded polygons based on their values. Here we can see the significant variation within classes through the use of the third dimension, and it serves the purpose of highlighting the massive spikes in activity in major urban centres. Used sparingly, such approaches can be useful, but great care is needed.

Mapping terrain

The third use case example here is mapping terrain. This category could also include mapping any value surface (e.g. pollution, rainfall, population density) but here we give the example of mapping elevation across the mountainous area which is home to Scotland's largest ski area, Cairngorm Mountain (Figure 5.8). In this example, ESRI's ArcScene and Ordnance Survey open data have been used to illustrate the rugged Highland terrain of the area in a simplified manner, with some other features such as woodland and lochs also shown. In a built environment context, particularly in hilly cities such as San Francisco, in the United States, and Sheffield, in the United Kingdom (where the authors are based), including terrain models in any 3D mapping is particularly important since it has a significant impact on human activity and issues such as transit routes and human interaction more generally. The first example shown in Figure 5.6, therefore, would ideally show San Francisco buildings draped over an elevation surface in order to more accurately portray the city.

Overall, then, the use of the third dimension in geovisualisation – particularly for those working in urban planning and built environment disciplines – can be a very effective tool. We just add a few words of caution to end. First, there needs to be some kind of rationale for using it – rather than just doing

Figure 5.8   *A 3D terrain map*

Cairngorm Mountain and Surrounding Area

it 'because we can'. Second, it must add value – otherwise using a traditional 2D approach is nearly always best. Third, we must be particularly careful that mapping in three dimensions does not cause so much visual occlusion that half the map cannot be seen. This is where web interactivity comes in particularly handy.

Pointless points and clueless choropleths?

Before we conclude this chapter, we want to briefly highlight two other potential pitfalls with geovisualisation. This issue has arisen in line with the growth in social media and the creation of maps by non-specialists, and has resulted in several online commentators bemoaning the use of techniques they view as wrong or even harmful. One is the case of unthinkingly plotting large volumes of points on a map ('pointless points') and the other is the issue of choropleth normalisation, or lack thereof, and how it can be problematic or misleading (hence 'clueless choropleths'). To illustrate this, we use the example of fire incidents in London.

One of the great things about the rise in open data in many nations is that we now have a large volume of spatial data with which to work. In London, we can now download massive spatial datasets with details of incidents attended by the London Fire Brigade service. The problem, of course, is that when we plot this on a map, it is just a massive visual data dump containing tens of thousands of points and this is neither informative nor useful (Figure 5.9). What we really need is some way to make sense of this data spatially so that we can compare the density of points at one location with the density of points elsewhere. This is where 'binning' comes in. This is just a way of aggregating point data to

Figure 5.9   *Fires in London: a not-very-useful dot map of almost 60,000 data points*

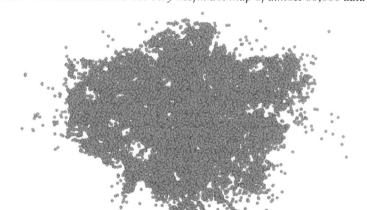

Pointless points? Not completely, but they are not really useful information at this stage.

Figure 5.10 *A slightly more useful representation of point density*

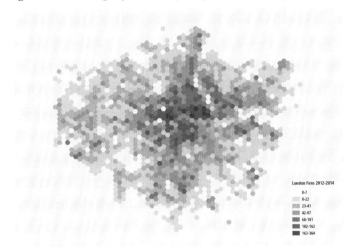

London Fires 2012-2014
0-7
8-22
23-41
42-67
68-101
102-162
163-364

That's better – now we have added some structure and it makes more sense.

standardised spatial units in order to make sense of it. A very popular approach is 'hex binning', using tessellated hexagons, as shown in Figure 5.10. This is an excellent example of the progression mentioned earlier in Chapter 4 between data and information, which can then give us knowledge.

Geovisualisation pioneer Waldo Tobler famously was not a fan of the now ubiquitous choropleth, saying 'I particularly abhor choropleth maps' but they remain a mainstay of GIS. Mapping values to coloured polygons, based on a variety of possible data classification systems is, however, here to stay and the choropleth has become even more widely used as the data and tools to make them have become more widely available. In case you did not know, the 'choro' part comes from the Greek word for land or territory and the 'pleth' part comes from the Greek word for multitude, which has a similar linguistic root to the English word 'plethora', which of course means a large or excessive amount of something.

As the use of the choropleth map has grown, we have witnessed more and more examples where the data is not displayed in an optimal manner. Usually, this means that people map raw totals to individual spatial units which have very different underlying populations. The end result is often a choropleth map that appears to show one thing but may in fact show another. The example of the New York City census tract population is a case in point. The map in Figure 5.11 shows a non-normalised map with raw population totals displayed for each census tract across the city, and the second shows the same data, normalised by area (i.e. to show population density). The map in Figure 5.11 is not 'wrong' as such, but since we use these kinds of maps to make comparisons between a large number of areas, it is problematic; that is, we are not really comparing like with like when we map this way. The problem arises because

Figure 5.11   *A non-normalised choropleth*

Figure 5.11   *A non-normalised choropleth*

Population

New York City

Census Tracts 2010

- 0 - 2,047
- 2,048 - 2,976
- 2,977 - 3,893
- 3,894 - 5,307
- 5,308 - 26,588

we are mapping a value to areas of differing geographical and population size, and although we can identify some patterns here, the map is rather confusing. We can tell, for example, that some areas of Staten Island have similar populations to census tracts in Queens or Manhattan, but that might just be because they are geographically larger. The underlying spatial structure and density may actually be very different, and in the context of studying and understanding the built environment, it is more likely that we are interested in density rather than raw population across spatial units of massively varying sizes. Hence, map in Figure 5.12 takes the same data but this time is it normalised by geographical area to show population density at the census tract level across New York City. This map is not necessarily more 'correct' than that in Figure 5.11, but it is significantly more informative and useful in many ways. The non-normalised version in Figure 5.11 shows high values for many tracts in Staten Island, giving the impression of 'high' population, but this is only because the spatial units are quite large here. The reality on the ground is that these areas are not very densely populated, as seen in the normalised version of the same map in Figure 5.12.

Figure 5.12   *A population density map – this makes more sense*

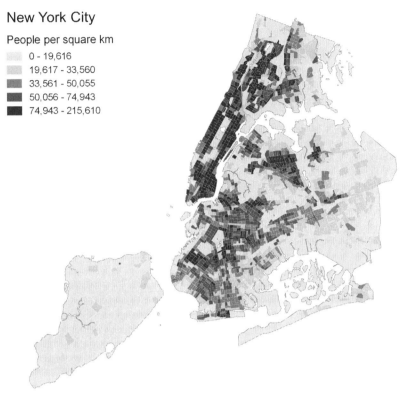

Population Density

New York City

People per square km

- 0 - 19,616
- 19,617 - 33,560
- 33,561 - 50,055
- 50,056 - 74,943
- 74,943 - 215,610

Our rule of thumb here is that you should *normally normalise*. But there are complications and exceptions. One example is crime data. In this case, we might be interested in the total number of crimes in an area, but dividing by geographical space here is not logical since it is not the same as population. Instead, it would make more sense to normalise by some other underlying variable, such as population at a certain point in time, or by number of businesses or homes. For this reason, some analysts like to present crime data on a per 1000 resident basis, but the problem with this is that it compares raw crime counts (which are fixed in space) with a population figure which almost certainly only really reflects where people sleep. The reality is that time of day is an extremely important intervening variable here and that if we wanted to normalise street crime in Manhattan, for example, we would have to be very sensitive to time of day since the population can vary enormously over 24 hours. If we want to normalise, then, we should be very clear about the data we are using as a denominator.

Sometimes the end user will be more interested in the absolute value of something, particularly if it relates to financial investment. An example here would be the total value of mortgage lending across London (Rae, 2014) where total figures are shown owing to the fact that (1) no demand variable can be specified due to a lack of data on the total number of applicants and (2) the intention was to show the total value of investment across small areas of London which do not vary greatly in terms of population. Such exceptions need to be carefully explained, however, and do not usually serve a general audience very well. We will give the final word here to Gretchen Peterson, who stated in her book *GIS Cartography: A Guide to Effective Map Design* that 'in most cases the appropriate choropleth method is to normalise your data' (Peterson, 2009, p. 88).

Augmented reality (AR) and virtual reality (VR): the future of GIS?

This is an introductory-level GIS textbook, so we are deliberately selective about what we include here, which means that we do not attempt to provide a comprehensive account of the entirety of GIS. Nonetheless, we think it is important that readers have some understanding of AR and VR within a GIS context. The best way to think of AR is as a technology that allows you to superimpose a computer-generated image on top of a user's view of the real world. A good example of this is AuGeo, from ESRI Labs, where users can view the real world through their mobile phone camera and see AR markers and information overlaid on screen to enhance (or augment) their view of the world. One example of a use for this in a real-world context would be in relation to showing hidden utilities or assets (such as underground cables used by utility companies). With an AR GIS app on the user's phone, they would be able to survey the scene in front of them and see geospatial markers overlaid on screen indicating the location of particular features they are interested in, such as where a pipe was located. Or, perhaps we want to create a walking tour for new students unfamiliar with our university. We could use AuGeo to create a guided route and use its AR features to display direction signs that students only see when viewing the world through their mobile phone. This is an emerging and quickly developing area of GIS, so we encourage interested readers to explore it further.

VR is not the same as AR, but it can be an even more immersive, spellbinding user experience. A common use case is in urban design, where we might wish to create a city tour for somewhere that we cannot visit in person. This is where technologies like Google Earth VR come in, since they allow us, in combination with VR headset technology, to explore virtual worlds in an immersive setting. The authors have had the opportunity to do this using an Oculus Rift headset on a VR tour of the city of Chicago and were blown away by the experience. The beauty of VR is that it opens up a whole new world of possibilities for exploring spatial data and interacting with it, in ways that were simply not possible a decade ago. Yet it is not quite fully mainstream within the world of GIS and, along with AR, is still viewed as being something of an emerging technology. However, with the speed at which technology is developing, we would expect AR and VR to move very quickly from the domain of 'next big thing' to everyday technology.

Conclusion

This chapter has attempted to cover some important topics in relation to geovisualisation, with practical examples to provide context. We have stated the case for geovisualisation and explained why it is important, and we have forwarded a set of purposes and principles which we hope readers will find useful. To end the chapter, we reiterate three important messages in the hope that these will resonate more widely with GIS analysts in the fields of urban planning and the built environment.

Geovisualisation as an 'appeal to the eye' – across all areas of scholarship, the lessons of the past are too easily forgotten and much of what appears new today has important historical antecedents. And so it is with geovisualisation. We therefore remind readers of Playfair's view of the visual approach as 'an appeal to the eye', albeit one that is demonstrably spatial. Some geovisualisation may in fact offend the eye(!) but if we follow the principles and purposes outlined in this chapter this is less likely.

Geovisualisation has several purposes – geovisualisation is not simply about making 'fancy maps' or using new software in complex ways. It can be used to explore data, to analyse it, to synthesise it and to present it. Many end users will only be aware of the presentation phase, but we hope that readers will understand its value more widely, particularly from an exploratory and analytical perspective.

In geovisualisation, simplicity is usually best – this does not mean that we think users should only map single variables or not attempt to perform technically complex tasks. Instead, we mean that the hard work of synthesis and analysis should be undertaken by the GIS expert, so that the cognitive load on the end user is lowered and the communicative power of the geovisualisation is maximised. This may be something as simple as normalising a choropleth, or it may be getting the orientation of a 3D representation just right so that visual occlusion is minimised.

Chapter 6

Mapping and the Built Environment: Some Guidance

Introduction

Following on from the previous chapter, on geovisualisation, this chapter provides a more practical guide to mapping in a real-world GIS environment. Whereas Chapter 5 focused more on general principles and approaches to mapping, in this chapter we provide specific examples of the kinds of use cases you are likely to come across in the fields of planning and the built environment. We attempt to cover the most important kinds of maps you may either make yourself or come across in your day-to-day work, and provide you with the kind of practical advice that can help you make better maps. This advice is not tailored to any particular piece of GIS software, but you will find that our 'how-to' approach can be implemented in any number of contemporary GIS applications, including QGIS, ArcGIS or MapInfo.

Our advice is based on the experience of the authors, who have used GIS for planning and the built environment for a combined total of more than four decades, going back to the late 1990s. This is important, because although the software we use may change from year to year, some fundamental principles remain the same, as we explain below. We also draw on the good advice of others, including Robert Kent and Richard Klosterman's (2000) article 'GIS and mapping: Pitfalls for planners' and Gretchen Peterson's (2009) book *GIS Cartography: A Guide to Effective Map Design*, both of which we suggest as recommended reading. Our experience is also leavened with the kind of practical experience that comes from working with planners and built environment professionals in the real world.

The rest of the chapter is divided up into sections based on different types of maps that you may encounter in professional practice or as a student of planning and the built environment. At the end of each section, we suggest key principles to follow for effective mapping. First of all, we discuss land cover maps of the type used in different contexts across the world. This kind of map is about categorising areas. In this section, we also touch on the use of colour. We then take a closer look at the choropleth map, an extremely common map type but one that is in our view often misused and misunderstood. The basic idea with the choropleth map is to assign a value (the 'pleth' part) to an area (the 'choro' part). We then discuss mapping the fabric of the built environment. Here we include maps relating to building footprints, including a kind of map that is also known as a 'figure-ground', particularly in an architectural context. This is a very effective way of representing the extent of the built-up and non-built-up area at a local level. We also discuss other relevant map types.

The penultimate section of the chapter focuses on map elements, such as labels, legends and scale bars. These seemingly 'little' items can play a big role in making our maps intelligible and useful, and, we argue, should not be over-looked. In the conclusions, we reflect on the different elements presented here and provide three key features of a 'good' map.

Land use maps

Maps which show what land is used for, what buildings there are, what land is zoned for or what is growing in a particular area have always had an important role to play in urban planning and the built environment. They help us under-stand the world in more detail and, depending on their type, they can tell us a great deal about ownership, function, future development potential and a host of other key factors. Given the central role such maps play, then, it is worth looking at an example of how we might map land use. It is also worth stating at the outset that maps which define land ownership in particular are known as cadastral maps. Most countries have a cadastre, many of which are publicly available, as in the Netherlands for example. The United Kingdom, on the other hand, does not have a cadastre and this can make it very difficult to find out who owns land.

An important point here is whether we are talking about 'land use' or 'land cover' (typically used in environmental mapping); the basic idea is that land is classified using some kind of nominal scheme. That is, each parcel of land is put into *named* categories rather than quantified. So, in a zoning map we might see land classified into categories such as 'Commercial', 'Light Industrial', 'Multi-Family Dwelling' and so on, as it is in the City of Vancouver. Or, in a land cover map, such as the European 'Corine' programme, land might be classified into many more categories, including 'Pastures', 'Peat Bogs', 'Green Urban Areas', 'Continuous Urban Fabric', 'Bare Rocks', 'Port Areas' and many more. In fact, the Europe-wide Corine Land Cover classification divides land into a total of 44 separate classes. Mapping such features in a clear and consistent manner can be difficult, particularly in areas where a large number of classes are pre-sent in a small area. The basic problem here relates to limitations on colour perception and how many different colours we can distinguish. Advice varies, but in general we recommend using no more than 12 different colours in a single map, but normally fewer.

This preamble provides useful context in relation to land use mapping because it points towards its purpose which, put simply, is to show what a particular area of land is used for. With a limited number of categories, it is possible to produce effective land use maps in colour. However, some land classifications have so many categories that it can be difficult for the viewer to distinguish between categories, such as in the case of Corine mentioned above.

However, it is usually the case that in urban studies and planning we are mapping much more localised areas using land use classifications devised by city planners and, in reality, this often means mapping a much lower number of categories than the 44 included in the EU's Corine Land Cover classification. A good example of this is the case of land use mapping in Brooklyn, New York, using MapPLUTO data published by the New York City Department of City Planning, as discussed previously in Chapters 5 and 6.

An additional important question we must pause to consider first, however, is the use of colour in thematic mapping. In this text, the maps you see are not reproduced in colour, owing to publishing requirements but the majority of the land cover mapping you will see or produce is in colour. However, land use mapping actually provides a useful example of both the difficulties of depicting a large number of categories *and* the difficulties of mapping when we are restricted in our use of colour. In the map in Figure 6.1, we can see a land use classification map, using MapPLUTO for part of Brooklyn in New York City (around 18th and 86th Street). However, when this is produced in black and white, as it is here, it is impossible to tell the difference between categories. In colour, the 12 different categories are distinguishable; though, because of the larger number of categories, some map readers may have difficulty telling some of them apart.

One way to get around the problem of having too many categories, *and* the problem of working without colour, is to use a small-multiple map approach.

Figure 6.1   *In greyscale, we cannot make much sense of these land use categories*

In this kind of map, several small maps are placed side by side so that users can compare the same area in relation to different variables. This is what is shown in Figure 6.2, the small-multiple map of Brooklyn, where we have mapped six of the MapPLUTO categories for Brooklyn and in each small map we can see the pattern associated with a different kind of land use.

The side-by-side nature of the layout makes comparison of land use types possible in black and white. For example, we can see that there are many more residential buildings (the top row) compared with mixed residential buildings, and we can also easily see that commercial and office buildings (bottom left map) are located along the major roads. This is a good way to overcome limitations

Figure 6.2 *Using a 'small-multiple' type approach we can make more sense of it*

One & Two Family Buildings

Multi-Family Walk-Up Buildings

Multi-Family Elevator Buildings

Mixed Residential & Commercial Buildings

Commercial & Office Buildings

Industrial & Manufacturing

if you are working in black and white, but it is also a useful approach even if you are able to use colour.

As with any map, the most important thing is that people can understand what you have produced and with land cover maps – because of the number of categories – this can be challenging. Therefore, we suggest the following guidelines if you are mapping land cover or land use in your own work.

- Use a maximum of 12 different categories when working in colour, and make sure that you select the colours very carefully (e.g. using the principles and tools developed by the ColorBrewer project).
- If working in black and white, consider using a small-multiple approach, as explained above.
- If you must use more than 12 colours, then we suggest careful analysis of the geography of your data so that similar colours are not located too close together. Careful consideration at this stage will make your maps more legible and increase their communicative potential.
- Make sure individual categories are clearly described in the legend. This is a very basic point, but it is sometimes overlooked.
- If you have one or two land use categories that comprise the majority of features, it is best not to use a very bold or dark colour to display them as this can overpower the other features that you want readers to be able to discern. A more muted colour is best in such cases.

Choropleth maps

The choropleth map is one of the most widely used map types. This is because it is easy to create in contemporary GIS software and readily understood by users. Or, at least that is the idea. The reality is a little more complex and the potential pitfalls quite considerable, so we take some time here to explain more. First used in the 1820s, it was named by American geographer John Kirtland Wright in his 1938 'Notes on statistical mapping' where he said: 'the term choropleth, which expresses the idea "quantity in area", is tentatively proposed' (Kirtland Wright, 1938, p. 14). Thus, we must always remember that the choropleth map is about *quantity* (the 'pleth' part of the name) and *area* (the 'choro' part). Areas are represented according to a value, yet this is not necessarily as simple as it sounds and there is potential for considerable confusion if the correct approach is not taken. Readers should also be aware that in recent years many people have begun to refer to choropleth maps as 'heat maps', a technically incorrect yet more appealing name. No matter what we call them, we need to exercise care in their composition and interpretation.

In order to demonstrate some of the challenges associated with choropleth maps, we will use the example of vacant housing data for at the counties of the lower 48 states of the United States. These counties vary widely in population, from more than 10 million people in Los Angeles County, California to just over

100 people in Loving County, Texas. Furthermore, counties also vary hugely in terms of the land areas they cover. The largest is San Bernardino County in California, and it covers more than 50,000 sq km (about 20,000 sq miles), which is larger than the Netherlands and twice as large as the state of Vermont. At the other end of the scale, New York County in New York (i.e. Manhattan) is just 59 square kilometres (about 22 square miles), yet it is the 20th most populous county in the United States. These kinds of variations are important, as we will see.

In the first map (Figure 6.3), we have a three-class choropleth map for the counties of the lower 48 US states. We have classified this in our GIS software using a 'quantile' classification, which is one of the options built in to the software. This classification puts an equal number of features in each category, so in this case we have 1036 counties in each statistical category. However, this would not be a good way to represent this data in reality. There are several reasons for this. First of all, we are mapping total numbers of vacant housing units onto a geography that varies wildly in terms of geographic area and population, as noted above. In effect, the pattern we see on the map is probably only showing which areas have a lot of housing and, by extension, a lot of people. This is essentially just a kind of three-class population map because the highest values are found in the areas with most people (and, by extension, the most houses). That fact that Maricopa County, Arizona has the highest number of vacant housing units (almost 228,000 in 2010) is not contextualised. Although this number is large relative to the others, we are not able to discern whether this number is proportionally much higher than in other areas.

If we want to see a more nuanced pattern of vacant housing that can properly inform us about the relative level of housing vacancy in each county, we need to standardise (or normalise) our choropleth map. This is what we have done

Figure 6.3   *Three-class choropleth – mapping totals (not a good idea)*

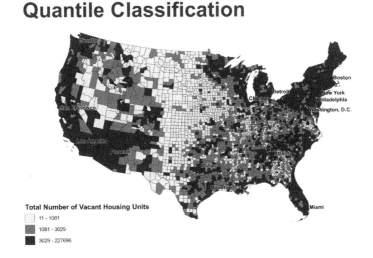

in the second map (Figure 6.4). Here, we have again used a three-class quantile classification so that there are 1036 counties in each of the three classes. This time, we see a very different and more meaningful map. The pattern is much more varied, with high values found throughout the United States and many areas which had high values on the totals map are now shown to have relatively low rates of housing vacancy. The vacancy rate in Maricopa County is just over 13% which now places it in the middle category.

This second map (Figure 6.4) is an improvement, but there is more to think about here. We are using a much more useful metric (percentage of vacant units rather than total units), but we need to think some more about the data classification method we have used, in relation to both the number of classes and the classification scheme we have selected. The key point here is that even if you use the default colour scheme suggested by your GIS software, this is still a choice and your data will reflect this. It may very well be the wrong choice. Therefore, we urge that great care is taken to represent data in the most appropriate way possible.

When it comes to classifying data, contemporary GIS packages such as MapInfo, ArcGIS and QGIS offer several different methods. You can manually define your data intervals. This might be useful if the data you are mapping needs to be scaled to match some pre-existing standard classification method that is widely accepted. An example here might be house prices, where the market is often segmented into prices at 50,000 or 100,000 price bands. Alternatively, we might select 'equal interval', in which our data is split into categories based on the range of values in our dataset. So, if we were working with a data range that went from 0 to 100 and opted to choose five equal intervals, we would have ranges of 0–20, 21–40, 41–60, 61–80 and 81–100. The intervals here are spaced apart equally, in contrast to the first example. Unlike the quantile classification there would almost certainly be a different number of

Figure 6.4   *Three-class choropleth – mapping percentages (much better)*

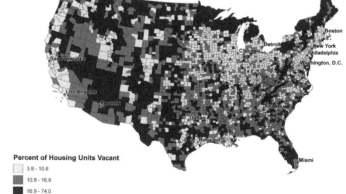

Percent of Housing Units Vacant

- 3.8 - 10.8
- 10.8 - 16.9
- 16.9 - 74.0

areas in each category, but for figures such as percentages this is a logical way to classify the data.

The classification set as the default in some GIS packages is 'natural breaks', which divides up a dataset based on so-called 'natural' groupings found in the data. This will vary between datasets, but the basic idea is that class breaks are placed so that features with similar values are grouped together. This approach is based on the Jenks optimisation method, devised by American cartographer George Jenks. There are a number of other, less-used data classification schemes built in to most software these days, but the classification methods mentioned above are the most commonly used and are therefore the focus here.

In order to show the effect of using different data classification methods for choropleth maps, we have mapped the housing vacancy percentage data four times in Figure 6.5, using a quantile (upper left), natural breaks (upper right), equal interval (lower left) and then manual classification (lower right). The question we may ask ourselves now is 'which one is right?'. The answer to this question in our view is that there can be no absolute 'right', but rather we should ask '*based on the underlying data, what is the most appropriate way to represent it?*'. This applies especially to choropleth maps but also to any kind of map or data visualisation.

In the quantile map, we see an equal number of counties in each category, which can tell us for example that a third of counties have a housing vacancy rate between 3.8% and 10.8%. However, many counties in this class are very small and the map appears to be dominated by the darker shades. Furthermore, the highest category has a very large range, extending from 16.9% to 74.0%. This is not very helpful because, although we know the darkest areas represent the highest third, we do not know if any given area in this class has a vacancy rate of 20% or 60%. The natural breaks map, on the other hand, presents a more nuanced view. Here, the data is split into three groupings based on the underlying distribution of vacancy rates. The lowest class extends from 3.8% to 16.4% and contains 2014 counties. The next class contains 877 counties and the highest category contains 217 counties. This is more useful, in that we now know the darkest areas have a vacancy rate of more than a third, but once again we are unable to tell which areas within this class have the highest values.

When working with variables like percentages or temperature, it can often be a good idea to use the equal interval data classification, as shown in the third map in Figure 6.5 However, because our data does not range from 0% to 100%, the classification method does not break the dataset up into categories of the same size and the final category begins at 51% rather than the more intuitive and useful 50%. Thus, in the final map, in Figure 6.6, we have used a manual classification so that we see counties with up to 25% vacancy rates, then those up to 50%, then over 50%. This, we would argue, is a much more effective and appropriate way of representing the data. First of all, it uses classes that intuitively make some kind of sense to the viewer. Second, it allows us to see that the vast majority of counties have a vacancy rate between 4% and 25%. Finally, it also allows us to see that very few counties have a vacancy rate of more than half.

Figure 6.5 *Different classification systems using the same dataset*

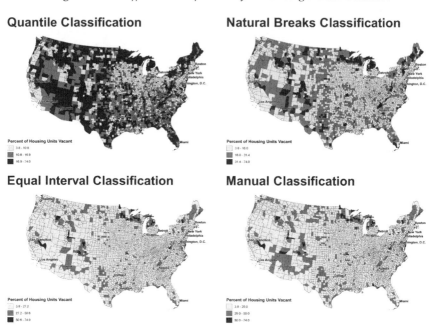

The only additional recommendation on classification we would make here is that it is very useful to add the number of areas in each category to the map legend, as we have done in the final map (Figure 6.6). This provides the reader with a statistical check on what they are looking at, and is particularly useful in cases where large geographic areas in a single class may dominate the map

Figure 6.6 *Manual classification using more 'intuitive' data ranges*

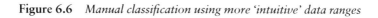

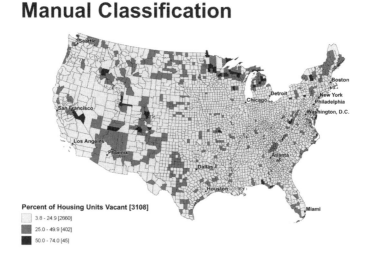

in terms of the proportion of total area they cover. You can do this manually in most GIS software or automatically at the click of a button in QGIS. The only other thing we have adjusted here is the decimal places in the map legend, so that each data range is mutually exclusive. Previously, it appeared that two areas in a different class could have a value of 25.0 (due to rounding), so to avoid this we have adjusted the legend manually so there is no statistical overlap between categories.

With this example we have shown that with a single dataset you can produce maps that look very different and, as a result, they may lead to different interpretations of the same data. In the original quantile classification, it appeared that a large proportion of the United States suffered from high housing vacancy rates. In a planning and urban studies context, this could lead to erroneous assumptions about a phenomenon, or confusion about what the data is telling us. In this case, with the final map (Figure 6.6) we can say that the vast majority of counties in the United States have a housing vacancy rate of less than 25% and we can also identify a group of 45 where the vacancy rate is above a half. However, even this approach is not perfect, so we end this section with some important points about choropleth maps that you should keep in mind.

- **Normally normalise** – in most cases, mapping the total number of a variable across space is not a particularly effective way of representing your data. However, if you are working with a geography that is uniform in area and population (e.g. a 1 km population grid) then mapping totals will make sense. In nearly all other cases, however, it is more useful to divide the total by a reference population. In the maps in Figures 6.5 and 6.6, we divided vacant housing units by the total number of housing units. However, there are times when it is unclear what the denominator should be. A good example of this is in crime mapping, where we may wish to show total numbers of street crimes by area and/or we do not have accurate data on daytime population.
- **Classification is critical** – as we have demonstrated above, the way we classify our data can have a massive impact on the final maps we produce, and, as a result, it can have a major impact on what conclusions people draw from our work. Therefore, always take time to consider carefully which classification scheme is most suitable for the data you are using. The default may not be the best choice. The number of classes also matters, and we recommend no more than seven for a choropleth map, but preferably five.
- **Spatial scale is important** – it is also important to be aware of the fact that when your geographic units vary widely in size, as in the case of US counties, it is easy for people to draw different conclusions from your maps. This is particularly true when large, predominantly rural counties take up a large proportion of a map (e.g., Figure 6.3) but may only account for a small percentage of the national total numerically. The opposite is also true for highly populated, urban areas which may be rather small in terms of area.

- **Details matter** – when people scrutinise your maps, as they will almost certainly do, it is important that the details are correct. In our example, we noted in Figure 6.6 that we adjusted the legend so that class boundaries did not overlap, and this is one example. We did not mention, however, that the total number of areas in the final map only adds up to 3107 rather than 3108. This is because of missing data for one county, and if we were publishing this work for a policy report, for example, we would have added a footnote to the map to explain.

Mapping the urban fabric: building footprints

Given that this book is about urban planning and the built environment, it is worth considering approaches to mapping the urban fabric. In recent years, more and more large-scale data has become available for cities across the world, from sources such as OpenStreetMap, or national mapping agencies. A good example of the latter comes from the United Kingdom, where the national mapping agency (Ordnance Survey) has made high-quality building footprint data publicly available, free of charge. The Ordnance Survey's *OS OpenMap – Local* data product includes building polygons for the whole of Great Britain, which means that planners, architects, urban planners and others are able to map the urban fabric with ease in GIS and other software.

Architects and urban designers will be familiar with this kind of map, which has long been known as a 'figure-ground' diagram, and which is basically a simple map that shows the relationship between built-up and non-built-up space. However, without access to data, such maps are difficult to produce. Thanks to Ordnance Survey, and other mapping agencies throughout the world, creating such maps, and others like them, has become much easier, so we offer some advice here on effective representation of the urban fabric. The key things to think about is simplicity and scale, as we explain here.

In Figure 6.7 and 6.8, we have represented an area of London in England using only building footprints, represented by a dark colour against a light background. The scale is also shown in the scale bar beneath each map. These maps were produced in a GIS at a scale of 1:75,000 but as you can see the two maps are not the same. This is because in the first map we have selected a line width of 0.5 mm and in the second we have used a line width of 0.1 mm. In the first map, in Figure 6.7, we can make out the general pattern of the built-up area, but it is only in the second map (Figure 6.8) where we get the detail and can see things more clearly. This serves as a very important, but simple, example of the ways in which small decisions can have big impacts when it comes to cartographic representation.

However, the impact of line width also varies by scale. In the maps in Figures 6.9 and 6.10, we have represented zoomed-in areas of London using the same approach – the maps on the left have a building outline width of 0.1 mm whereas the maps on the right have a building outline width of 0.5 mm.

In Figure 6.9, produced at a scale of 1:25,000 we can see differences between how well defined the buildings are, but it is not as clear a difference as in Figure 6.8. The map on the right is clearly darker and gives the impression that buildings cover a larger area than they actually do. In Figure 6.10, line widths of 0.1 mm (left) and 0.5 mm (right) are again used, but, at the 1:5000 scale, it is almost impossible to tell the difference.

We use this brief example here for two reasons. First, it highlights the potential utility of new data sources for urban planners and those working in built environment disciplines who previously had little knowledge of these kinds of maps, which can be a very effective way of illustrating the extent, form and density of the urban environment. Second, it highlights the impacts our technical choices can have on our maps and the way in which this can have a negative or positive impact on legibility. This might seem trivial, yet it is extremely important, and we therefore urge readers to take great care when producing such maps. Done well they can be an extremely effective way of representing the built environment, but without sufficient care they have the potential to mislead.

Figure 6.7   *An example of how line width can affect your map (see Figure 6.8 for comparison)*

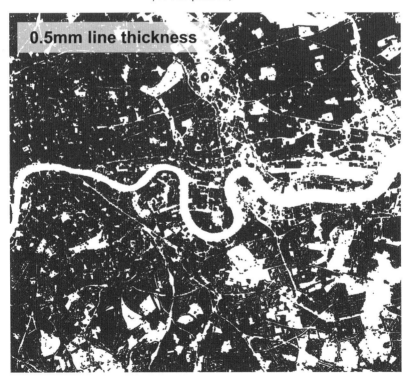

5,000 metres

Figure 6.8   *An example of how line width can affect your map (see Figure 6.7 for comparison)*

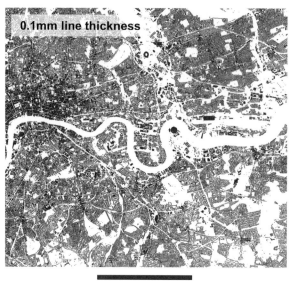

5,000 metres

Figure 6.9   *Comparison of line widths mapped at a scale of 1:25,000*

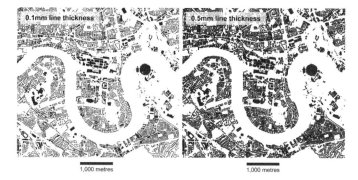

Figure 6.10   *Comparison of line widths mapped at a scale of 1:5000*

We have touched on mapping building footprints here because it is a very effective and simple way to illustrate the relationship between the urban fabric and the non-built-up areas. Furthermore, it has become increasingly possible, owing to newly available data across the world, including the Ordnance Survey data used above. To finish, we suggest three simple principles for effective mapping of the urban fabric.

- The use of dark shades is best, in order to emphasise the contrast, since that is exactly what such maps are intended to do. We prefer a very dark grey (e.g. RGB 34, 34, 34 or #222222).
- The colour of the polygon fill should match the outline colour. If this is not the case, it can create more visual 'clutter' and be more confusing for the viewer.
- Line thickness is critical. At a very local scale you may not notice the difference, but, as we have seen, it can have a significant impact when zoomed out. Therefore, we suggest a narrow line thickness, perhaps 0.1 mm.

Other types of map

There are many different map types we could potentially use as planners and urbanists. We have referred to most of them throughout this text, so here we provide a short round-up of different map types that you may either see or want to use in your own work. The first map type we want to highlight is the proportional symbol map. As the name suggests, this type of map sizes symbols according to a numerical variable, as in the example in Figure 6.11 where the number of new terraced houses sold in London at the postcode level between 2010 and 2015 is shown. It allows us to see both spatial pattern and quantity, but a potential drawback exists where there are multiple values located close together, as we see in Figure 6.11 in some cases. Nonetheless, such maps can be useful.

The use of 3D maps is now becoming more common, thanks to increased data availability and improved software and hardware. However, we would suggest that readers need to think carefully about how and when they might use three dimensions when mapping. It can look very appealing, but it does not always add value. There is certainly a 'wow factor' associated with 3D maps, but this must be balanced against the rationale for using them in the first place. So, for example, if we wish to model the urban environment in three dimensions in order to provide an overview of what a city looks like, as in Figure 6.12, this might provide the kind of additional information that, say, a building footprint map does not provide, since it can show the additional variable of the height of buildings. This example covers part of Greater Manchester in England, with parts of the districts of Trafford, Salford and Manchester visible.

Likewise, if we were mapping population density using a 1 km grid dataset (as in the next example), the use of 3D will allow us to see more differentiation within classes in a dataset and allow us to see where the highest values

Figure 6.11   *A proportional symbol map*

New Build Housing Sold in London
Terraced houses (3,067 - 7.1% of total)

are, in a way that a flat representation cannot. This is another case when the use of the third dimension can add value. It is also an example of a kind of choropleth map where the data has not been normalised, due to the fact that each unit is the same size (1 km sq) and therefore the denominator is the same for every cell.

Another type of map of use to those working in urban planning and the built environment is the flow map. There are many variations on this kind of map, but the basic idea is to show the connections between places in relation to some kind of 'flow'. Typically, this will be some kind of human movement, such as

Figure 6.12   *A 3D representation of buildings in Greater Manchester*

Figure 6.13 *A 3D representation of population density in south-east England*

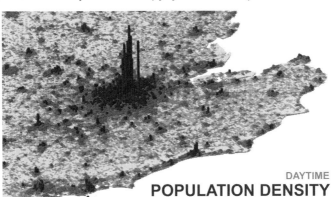

DAYTIME
POPULATION DENSITY

commuting or migration, but it could also relate to the movement of goods, or even the migration patterns of birds. No matter what, it is about showing the connections between places and a good example here is the analysis of commuting patterns. We have provided an example of this in Figure 6.14, where

Figure 6.14 *A flow map of commuting in the San Francisco Bay Area*

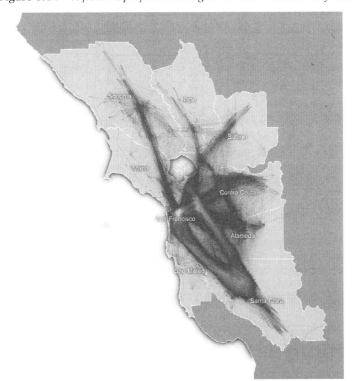

flow lines connect the commuting origins and destinations in the nine counties of the Bay Area around San Francisco in the United States. This map shows all census tract to census tract commutes (of 10 or more) as straight lines between origins and destinations.

There are many, many other kinds of maps in existence today, but we have only included the most relevant ones here since our focus is on GIS for planning and the built environment. Furthermore, the potential of interactive mapping on the web has created a whole new wave of cartographic material, though the underlying principles of cartography have not changed. What has changed is that we are now in a situation where it is easier to obtain the data and software necessary to make maps. Thus, we concur with cartographer Kenneth Field (2018), who says that 'making maps is easy' but also that 'making great maps is hard'. Great care is needed in the creation of maps, particularly when they are to be used to inform policy.

One further point that we need to emphasise here is that all map types have their drawbacks. The choropleth map, for example, can conceal considerable variation within classes, and some users can find it hard to distinguish between colours. Land cover maps often suffer from trying to map too many categories, and proportional symbol maps can end up looking like a giant 'data dump' if we are not careful. Yet the power of maps to inform and educate is perennial, and their utility remains very high. Besides the 'big picture' issues we have raised here, however, we also need to think about the details, and this is what we now turn to in the penultimate section in relation to different map elements.

Map elements

Beyond the main content of the map itself, it is also very important to think about the details. In fact, if we do not think carefully about the little things, then the maps we produce may not educate and inform in the way we intend. Therefore, it is important at this stage to discuss the various map elements that help complete maps and make them powerful communication devices. In this respect, we agree with Cynthia Brewer (2005) who emphasises the need to think about the connection between map content and end use. Here we think of this as being embodied in the principle that 'context defines content', in that the context within which the map is produced should have a strong influence on the content, and the effects of this idea can be seen in the final maps we produce.

An example of this might be in a local map where we simply wish to show the relationship between the built and unbuilt environment, as we have in Figures 6.7 and 6.8. In this example, things like direction are not absolutely critical, but scale might be, so we have added a simple scale bar in those cases. However, if we are producing maps for navigation, the omission of a north arrow would be a very grave mistake. There are many people who say that every map *must* have a scale bar, north arrow, title and perhaps some other elements. We would instead argue that this is usually the case, but that it is not a universal rule. To some extent, it depends on end use, map format (e.g. static map vs. interactive map), and a variety of other factors. Before concluding this chapter, we run through a selection of important map elements and comment on them each individually. This is offered as guidance in the context of GIS and spatial analysis for planning and the built environment. For general advice on this topic, we suggest readers refer to Chapter 3 of Peterson's excellent *GIS Cartography: A Guide to Effective Map Design*.

- **Map title** – certainly, it is always a good idea to have a title for any maps you produce. With modern GIS, the question is whether we wish to embed the title in the image file we save during our work, or whether we wish to simply caption the map with a title later – for example, if it is to be used in a report. Our advice here is that, in general, it is always a good idea to include the title in the map, and that it should be short and simple so that readers can understand what your map is about. In terms of placement, top left is our preference, though lower centre is also an appropriate option.
- **Scale bar** – usually this is an important map element, because we are mapping geographical features and distance is normally an important factor. Unless it is absolutely not necessary (e.g. a global choropleth map of per capita income by country would hardly be diminished by the absence of a scale bar and it would serve little purpose), we would always recommend including a scale bar. The units used should be understandable by the end user. So, if your audience are not familiar with the metric system, using kilometres is likely to confuse – even if you believe it is more scientific. However, a good compromise is to use both, if possible.
- **Legend (also known a key)** – this is also nearly always essential. The key question here is 'how will readers know what individual features represent'? If you are mapping trees, and use a tree icon for individual features, it may not be necessary to explain further, but the vast majority of maps will require a legend that can serve as a point of reference. Most modern GIS software will automatically generate a legend, in a vertical format with symbols to the left and descriptions to the right, and this normally works well. However, it is also possible to manually draw legends if the default options do not prove satisfactory. A really important thing here is to give your individual map legend items intelligible names so that people can understand what they represent. If you are not careful, in some GIS packages the technical layer name (e.g. *buildings_nyc_mappluto_v17.shp*) can end up in the legend, and this is never a good look.
- **North arrow** – as noted above when we discuss map elements, this is not always essential (the case of the global choropleth map of per capita incomes is again a relevant example) but at the same time it is normally best to include some indication of direction if this is at all important to the underlying purpose of the map. So, as with the scale bar, we would suggest nearly always including this map element. One note of caution, though. Try to avoid the

temptation to add a highly embellished, 'olde worlde' style north arrow unless you are trying to recreate a historical map. Simplicity almost always enhances legibility, so a simple north arrow is best, placed in one corner, or perhaps beside the scale bar.

- **Inset map** – a key consideration when mapping is whether the people looking at your map will know the location of the map area in a wider context. It may not always matter, but if we were producing a map of a hurricane path in Florida, for the BBC in the United Kingdom (see 'Authorship, copyright, sources' below), it would be wise to include a locator map, owing to the fact that not all viewers may be familiar with the location featured in the main map view. This kind of additional information can be really helpful, but it is sometimes overlooked and can lead to confusion.
- **Authorship, copyright, sources** – we have grouped these three elements together because they are important, and related. If you are producing maps as an individual for a client, for example, adding your name to the map may serve two useful purposes. First, it indicates who made the map so that future viewers would know who to contact if they need further information or additional mapping. Second, it provides the mapper with proper attribution, particularly in an age when images can be shared so easily online. We must also be careful to add any necessary copyright notices to our maps. Even with the rise of open data, most data providers require some kind of copyright or attribution notice. This may not be a formal copyright notice, as is necessary with Ordnance Survey data in Great Britain, but may instead be a citation relating to the source of your data. A good set of questions to ask yourself when producing a map is whether someone viewing the map would be able to (1) discern who made it; (2) identify what data were used; and (3) copy or replicate it without permission?

These are the most important map elements to consider, though there are many other less important ones (such as adding company logos, additional descriptive text or a page border), but in our view it is best only to add the necessary items, and to do so in a way that minimises clutter. In this respect, it can often be a good idea to follow a general principle of 'map in the middle, elements in the margins' so that the central focus is always the map.

Conclusion: characteristics of a 'good' map

In this chapter, we have tried to provide some practical guidance to help readers understand better how they might produce 'good' maps. Yet, as we have seen, there are many potential pitfalls on the journey to creating good maps and there is a lot to think about. The question of what makes a 'good' map is of course also open to a degree of interpretation. However, if we make careful choices and devote sufficient thought to the process, it is possible to produce informative, impactful and highly useful maps for urban planning and the built environment. This requires going beyond the point-and-click functions of any particular GIS package and requires us to use human decision making.

To put this in more concrete terms, if we are thinking about a land use map, then a 'good' map will be one where people can distinguish one category of land use from another, understand what those categories are and understand where they are. If we are thinking about a choropleth map, a 'good' map will normally be one where the data has been normalised so that the differences between areas can be compared on an equal basis, but we must also be able to distinguish between colours and the classification scheme we use must also be appropriate for the data we are using. If we are simply mapping building footprints at the scale of an entire city, we may have fewer choices to make, but here the appropriate use of colour, line thickness and the addition of a scale bar are essential properties of what we can think of as a 'good' map. The point here is that the elements of what makes a 'good' map can vary between map types, audience, end use and even the media we view maps on (e.g. paper vs. screen, mobile vs. monitor). Nonetheless, we think it is possible to distil from this three key principles in relation to the characteristics of what makes a 'good' map, and we end with these.

- **Simplicity.** We believe all 'good' maps have a significant element of simplicity to them in that they will have created a highly legible map based on the underlying complexity of the real world. This could mean only including on our maps the essential data and information, and iteratively removing unnecessary map elements or embellishments. This principle applies to map content, but also to map elements so that – for example – legend names are simple but intelligible, map titles are not overly long and colours have been chosen appropriately (e.g. using ColorBrewer).
- **Appropriate for end use.** This is an important principle, since it dictates that the maps we produce should be created with the end use in mind. If we are creating maps for a specialist audience of transport planners, then a more technical-looking map may be appropriate, but the same is not true if we are producing a map for consultation with the general public. There is something of a paradox here in that the definition of 'good' is context-dependent not on the content or style of the map but in relation to the end user. This applies to *who* the map is for, but also in relation to *how* it will be viewed, in terms of the media it will be displayed on.
- **Adds value.** This may be an obvious point, but a 'good' map is also one that adds value over and above what could be achieved without a map. Sometimes, however, the 'where' in data is not the most important element and another form of visual communication may be more appropriate. If we are mapping the results of a national election, for example, geographic voting patterns will always be important, and maps are an essential part of reporting results. If geographic location is not relevant, then a map is probably not the best approach. A good example here would be if you were comparing beer consumption per capita for European countries. A simple bar chart, ordered from highest consumption to lowest, would illustrate the

pattern in the data very effectively, but a map would not because of the highly variable size of countries and the fact that it would be difficult to see the underlying data, whether we used a choropleth or proportional symbol map. When location is the most important element of the data we are using, or even just an important detail, then a map can add value, so long as your data is accurate and you make good choices in relation to map type and layout. Yes, by all means make maps – but do your best to make sure they add value!

Chapter 7

'Everything Is Related to Everything Else': Understanding Spatial Analysis

Introduction

The real power of GIS comes from spatial analysis, rather than just making maps. It is possible to do spatial analysis and not make any maps, but the two most often go hand in hand. Many modern software applications can make maps, but with a fully fledged geographic information system we can perform the kinds of spatial analyses that can help us answer location-based questions such as 'what is nearby?', 'how far away is it?' or 'where should we build it?'. In this chapter, we explore such questions in the context of urban planning and the built environment. This means that we do not cover every possible use case for spatial analysis, but we do highlight examples relevant to our field. Before we do this, it is useful to consider the fundamental property underlying all spatial analyses: that of geographic space itself. We deal with this and other questions in the remainder of the chapter, but we want readers to remember that when we perform analyses with spatial data we are operating in a world of models and assumptions, whereas the social and physical worlds we often analyse can have their own priorities and can act in rather unpredictable ways. The 'best' location for a new supermarket may be easy to determine based on spatial analysis alone, but this will undoubtedly come into conflict with competing local interests of residents and existing store owners – not to mention environmental considerations. The optimal solution in such cases therefore requires a careful mix of spatial analytical and people-centred decision making.

Put simply, in any form of spatial analysis, we just need to remember that techniques and methods at our disposal should be thought of as a powerful toolset, rather than an answer to the question of why the world is the way it is in the first place, or how it should be. This may seem like a very obvious thing to say, but we think it is important to highlight the issue at a time when the capabilities of computer-based spatial analysis are so computationally advanced and the results often so captivating. It may be the case that to understand the world fully we need to do spatial analysis, but, equally, a keen researcher might find that just talking to a few people will provide better answers. However, once you establish that taking a spatial analytical approach is a good way to proceed, there are a number of different things you ought to consider, as we explain below.

We do not attempt to provide a step-by-step guide to spatial analysis here, since there are many other good resources designed for this purpose. Instead, this chapter aims to highlight the power and value of spatial analysis by putting it into context. First of all, we look at the issue of Tobler's 'First Law of Geography', so often cited but too little discussed, particularly in relation to how Waldo Tobler himself conceived of it. Following this, we then consider what 'space' actually is, why 'spatial is special' and why spatial analysis might be appropriate. We then look more closely at some spatial analysis operations in relation to specific techniques. Following this, we reflect on the fundamental questions of distance and connection. Our conclusions report that we firmly believe in the power of spatial analysis, but they also serve as a reminder that it can rarely answer the most important social science question of all: that of 'why'. But without spatial analysis in planning and built environment disciplines, fundamental questions relating to location would be much more difficult to answer.

Tobler's 'First Law of Geography'

In 1970, the Swiss-American geographer and polymath Waldo Tobler published a paper entitled 'A computer movie simulating urban growth in the Detroit region' in the journal *Economic Geography*. On the first page of his paper, he said that 'as a premise, I make the assumption that everything is related to everything else' (Tobler, 1970, p. 234). He is careful to point out that this may apply to time as well as space, and he goes on to state: 'I invoke the first law of geography: everything is related to everything else, but near things are more related than distant things' (1970, p. 236). This statement has since become known as the 'First Law of Geography'. Anyone who has studied human geography should be familiar with this premise since it is a fundamental principle of spatial analysis, though it is less well known outside the discipline. It is perhaps both obvious and logical, but like any law there are exceptions. One of the most obvious examples of the First Law in action is house prices. Normally, houses close to each other are similar in value. We can see this in the way poor and rich areas are clustered in cities. A notable exception to this may be where, for example, a river or railway line cuts through a city and on either side house prices are significantly different. Such areas may be 'near' in geographic space, but in the social world they may actually be miles apart and, therefore, very different in monetary value.

As a general principle, the First Law of Geography is very useful. It serves as a reminder of the fundamental properties of how phenomena are organised across geographic space. This applies to the social world, but also to the physical world – for example, think of soil types, tree species or weather patterns: areas nearby each other are more likely to be similar. For further discussion and debate around the First Law, it is worth referring to a set of papers from 2004 which discuss the concept from the perspective of whether it is 'A Big Idea for a Small World' (Sui, 2004). The authors of this book encourage readers to take a critical view of such 'Laws', as Tobler himself might, but also to understand that the First Law does serve as a very useful reference point to how the social and spatial world is organised.

Less well known, perhaps, is that Waldo Tobler also proposed a 'Second Law of Geography', which relates to the first. Tobler stated: 'my second law of geography asserts that "the phenomenon external to [a geographic] area of interest affects what goes on in the inside; a sufficiently common occurrence as to warrant being called the second law of geography"' (Tobler, 2004, pp. 308–309). This also makes sense when we think about it in the real world. Consider, for example, the case of a rich neighbourhood surrounded by areas of high crime. The residents of the wealthy neighbourhood will in many cases change their behaviour and actions based on what exists beyond their boundaries. This may mean taking extra security precautions, establishing a gated community, purchasing weapons for protection or changing their travel patterns. This is obviously a simplified example, but there are many examples of this across the world, particularly in developing countries where urban densities lead to rich and poor living in close proximity.

In urban planning and the built environment, the First Law is particularly important. The principle of 'nearness' is, one could argue, what it is all about. For example, a new housing development must be near to transport infrastructure like major road and rail links, otherwise it would not be viable economically or socially. A new office development must be optimally located so that workers can access it easily and also so that the use of space is maximised relative to the investment. Similarly, a new rail line must be planned so that its stations are near, and accessible, to as many people as possible. Geographic space is, then, an absolutely central part of what we study in the built environment, but before going any further we think it is useful to pause to consider what 'space' actually is before we proceed to say why it is particularly important.

What on earth is space?

Before going on to introduce and discuss spatial analysis, it is first necessary to spend a little time explaining what we mean by geographic 'space' and why the analysis of it requires a special set of techniques. At a very basic level, we can think of space as land. Space is the surface of the earth, on which social interactions take place, and on which buildings are constructed, roads are built and development is planned. In this sense, however, space is also more than just land; it is the geographic areas we inhabit, the public spaces we enjoy, the contested canvas on which we plan and build. It is a physical thing, but it is also social. That is, geographic space is imbued with all kinds of value – from the social and physical to the cultural and symbolic. Just think of how we might have a mental map of a town or city based on our experiences of it as a child, or how much we value beautiful landscapes over barren ones. In the context of geographic information systems, however, it is modelled and simplified in order that it can be represented digitally. As we describe in Chapter 4, this can be displayed in vector format as points, lines and polygons or as a continuous raster surface of square cells. Of course, there are many different ways to describe, explain and understand space, but in the context of this book *we think of it as a geographic surface on which activities take place – from the scale of individual buildings to entire countries, or beyond*. We would caution the reader, however, to remember that any spatial analysis we conduct with GIS – no matter how methodologically robust – will never be able to explain things fully. Our tools are no doubt powerful, but they are also partial. A particularly interesting and innovative approach to the understanding of space in the built environment can be seen in Box 7.1, where we highlight the work of Space Syntax.

Box 7.1   Space Syntax

Space Syntax is a London-based planning, architecture and research consultancy that specialises in analysing the built environment in relation to the concept of 'space syntax'. Their mission is to 'enhance the social, economic and environmental performance of buildings and urban places by developing, disseminating and applying a science-based, human-focused approach' to planning, design and operation. This may sound rather abstract, but within this mission is an implicit recognition of the importance of space and why the spatial layout of buildings and places exerts a powerful influence on human behaviour. Crucially, as they say on their website:

> Space connects or segregates; brings people into social and economic relationships or keeps them apart; helps people save time or consigns them to carbon-intensive lifestyles; enhances real estate value or damages investments; increases safety or encourages criminal behaviour.

Within this statement we can see something of Tobler's First Law, but also his Second Law. Integral to the idea of Space Syntax is the notion of relative connectivity and how parts of the built environment relate to one another. This is based on three basic notions of space. First, an 'isovist' idea of space is about what can be viewed from any given location. Second, the idea of axial space (from the work of Bill Hillier at the Bartlett School of Architecture at University College London) is also critical. This conceives of space in relation to sight lines and possible paths. Finally, the idea of convex space is part of the space syntax view of space. In this view, space is simply a void within which all areas within a space are visible to all other points within it. These principles have, taken together, been used by Space Syntax in a series of innovative projects to transform the built environment in cities across the world, including Beijing, Changchun, Jeddah, Darwin and London. A key feature of the Space Syntax approach is that it can be deployed at a variety of scales, from within single buildings to entire cities, and beyond. For more on this approach to space, see http://www.spacesyntax.com.

The definition of space as *a geographic surface on which activities take place – from the scale of individual buildings to entire countries* then raises a related question: how can space be measured? In the vector GIS model, space can be measured through the use of geographic coordinates to identify points, lines or polygons. This allows us to measure areas (e.g. hectares or square miles), the lengths of lines (such as roads) and the distance between two or more points. In the case of raster data, it can be measured through the assignment of values to individual cells of data, which cover a continuous surface. This distinction is important in spatial analysis since the tools we use to analyse vector and raster data are often different, and this stems from the way we define and measure space in the first place. These issues are considered later in the chapter when we discuss different spatial analysis techniques.

But, of course, 'space' is not some kind of blank canvas, and how we measure it and analyse it depends on both its innate characteristics and its specific location. It also depends on the values people place on it in relation to use or sale. A classic example here might be an urban park, such as Central Park in New York City. This public park occupies a prime location at the heart of one of the world's great cities, where the incredibly high land values are expressed in the built environment through skyward structures which form a kind of wall round Central Park. The point here is that the nature and value of spaces depend not only on what is on them (e.g. meadows or skyscrapers) but also in relation to what is nearby; always a key consideration in urban planning. This kind of question is an inherently spatial one, and one that is apt to be explored further with spatial analysis methods in GIS.

Before we move on to consider why a spatial analytical approach is both appropriate and necessary for planning and the built environment, we want to consider one more issue related to the nature of space. Take as an example one square kilometre of data covering part of the Rocky Mountains. If we used a 1 km × 1 km 'cookie-cutter' approach to measure the land from above, we would end up with a parcel that had four 1 km long sides. However, because the land within this area is folded, sloped and peaked, the actual land area is likely to be much more than a single square kilometre. This kind of 'creased rug' effect may seem trivial if we are just grazing a flock of sheep, but if we are planning for development then it is a question we must consider. There are a variety of different surveying methods we could use to deal with this issue, but that is not the point here. We just want readers to understand that the idea of space as an uncomplicated blank canvas is one that needs to be treated with caution, even if it does appear that way when we analyse space in a GIS.

Why spatial analysis for planning and the built environment?

When people talk of residential or commercial real estate, it is often said that there are three things that matter: location, location and location. So it is hardly surprising that in a book about planning and the built environment we would be talking about spatial analysis since it is, fundamentally, all about location. Here we consider why it is particularly important and useful in these disciplines, before we go on to explore the topic in more detail. Put simply, where buildings and infrastructure are located is the most important thing. If we were to open a new Tam's Burgers restaurant in Los Angeles, we would want it to be optimally located in relation to our target customer demographic. If we construct a new freeway we want the maximum possible number of people to be able to use it, and if we build a new town we need to make sure that it is laid out properly internally but also accessible to other towns and cities nearby. In the past, these issues would have been tackled using a variety of cartographic, surveying and analytical techniques, but today we can perform such tasks with spatial analysis in a GIS. However, the basic principles of spatial analysis are not unique to geographic information systems and our first example below briefly illustrates this.

In post-war Britain, there was a need to build new homes, replace slum housing and provide modern infrastructure. A city where this was particularly pressing was in Glasgow, Scotland's largest city. Bombed heavily in the Second World War and chronically overcrowded in the central districts, it needed new places to accommodate its overflowing population. Part of the answer to this was its involvement in the New Towns programme, which operated in three main waves in the post-war era. One such new town was to be Cumbernauld, just over 10 miles to the north-east of Glasgow city centre and – it was hoped – home to 70,000 new residents. Cumbernauld was designated as a site for a New Town in 1955 and the first residents moved in during 1958. The choice of location for this new town was not a point-and-click exercise in a GIS, but instead the result of a series of carefully considered geographic, social and political decisions, in addition to traditional surveying and mapping techniques. As we can see from the map in Figure 7.1, this was then presented as an 'Outline Plan' in much the same way that a modern GIS would produce, yet the underlying techniques were more rudimentary in technical terms; though some might argue they were also more carefully considered.

However, all of this was presupposed on there being space available to site such a large new development, and this is a key point. When conducting spatial analysis, whether using traditional paper-based methods in the case of Cumbernauld or state-of-the-art spatial analysis software, the user must remain aware that the surface of the earth is complex, imperfect and laden with value – cultural, social, economic and more. The planners of the New Town era in the United Kingdom knew this, and even without GIS software were able to conduct quite complex spatial analyses to help support their decisions on questions of 'where'. This means that key questions of location such as 'where should we build it?' may have a simple answer in theory, but finding an optimal solution in practice requires us to go beyond the domain of the abstract spatial analytical model and into the realm of human decision making. That is to say, spatial analysis and GIS have been incredibly useful tools in planning and the built environment, but they work best when we accept that we live in a complex political, social and economic context. The very mixed legacy and

Figure 7.1   *Outline Plan of Cumbernauld New Town in Scotland*

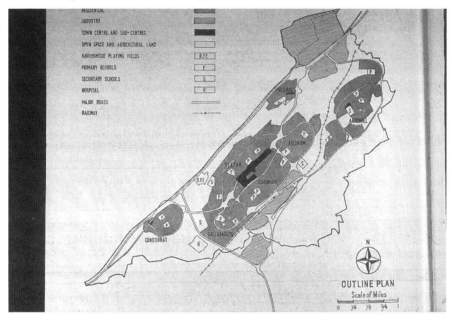

Outline Plan of Cumbernauld (JR James Archive, University of Sheffield CC-BY)

reputation of the New Towns programme in the United Kingdom are a good example of this. Some later new towns, such as Milton Keynes (50 miles north-west of London), are widely accepted as successful examples of urban planning, while others are derided as planning failures. This is not the result of a lack of technological sophistication or the absence of GIS and spatial analysis, but a pertinent reminder that planning and the built environment are inherently complex activities that, at times, defy expectation or explanation.

Taking a different example, from the modern day, the question of how far one can travel for work is an inherently spatial one, and one that can be answered using a series of more complex spatial analysis techniques. A good example of this is the 'Mapumental' project and toolkit developed by MySociety, a not-for-profit social enterprise based in the United Kingdom. Their analysts sought to use public transport data to answer the question of how far you can travel within certain time thresholds at certain times of day, based on large open transport datasets. This is particularly useful for people seeking employment, who need to know how long it might take them to get to a new job on public transport. Furthermore, it is also useful for people seeking to move house who want to check whether their new home would be within reach of an existing job within a viable time frame (e.g. 45 minutes). In the example in Figure 7.2, we selected a destination postcode (M16 0RA) in the Greater Manchester area and then set the Mapumental time slider to 45 minutes, so that we can see the geographic footprint within which we can reach this destination on public transport in 45 minutes. We can modify the preferred arrival or destination

Figure 7.2   *Mapumental map of 45-minute travel zone to M16 0RA in
Greater Manchester*

times to take account of rush hour traffic, for example, but the end result is
always an area that looks something like a large 'splodge' of light colour on an
otherwise dark map. You can see more isolated pockets of accessibility along
key rail corridors (rendered as circles on the left of Figure 7.2), and the non-
symmetrical nature of the light coloured area is testament to both the complexity of the underlying street network in Manchester and the different modes of
public transport which it analyses (bus, train and tram). We discuss this type of
analysis further in Chapter 8.

   This second example is also a good way of understanding Tobler's First
Law from a slightly different perspective, because 'nearness' and 'distance' in
this case have to be viewed differently – they are not always the same thing.
Some parts of Manchester that are close to M16 0RA are actually much further away in time by public transport than we might expect based on their
geographical location alone. This topic is covered later in the chapter, but for
now it is worth remembering that geographical proximity is not the only kind
of 'nearness' that matters in planning and the built environment. Network
accessibility is also particularly important; and in many cases it is actually
more important.

   The two brief examples presented above – British New Town location planning and travel time analysis for public transport – are at opposite ends of a
spectrum in relation to technical sophistication, but they belong to the same
family of spatial analysis problems that urban planners and built environment
professionals have grappled with for decades. Issues related to proximity, availability of infrastructure, what is nearby and other inherently spatial problems
are absolutely central here. So, to answer the question in the title of this chapter,

the reason that we use GIS and spatial analysis in planning and the built environment is that it can help us answer the perennial questions of our disciplines, including but not limited to:

• Where is the ideal site for a new development?
• How many people live within a distance of a specific location?
• What is nearby?
• How connected are places?
• How clustered is a particular phenomenon?
• What is the commuter footprint of a city?

The next section of this chapter looks at some of these questions in relation to key GIS methods, and Chapter 8 examines in more detail those questions relating to network analysis – a more specialised branch of GIS. These methods are at the heart of spatial analysis and, whether we know it or not, were most likely involved in the decision-making process which led to the store you buy your groceries from being located exactly where it is.

Spatial analysis methods: what and how?

Answering the questions posed in the previous section is no trivial task. Thankfully, the tools available to us in contemporary GIS packages make them relatively easy to perform, so in this section we will look at some specific spatial analysis methods in order to understand more about what they are and how they are implemented. These can be carried out using popular proprietary GIS packages like ArcGIS and MapInfo or free, open source solutions like QGIS. The important thing to remember is that we should think of GIS not as a specific software package, but rather as a set of spatial analysis tools which help us answer particular geographic questions. Our software will always evolve and improve, but the underlying fundamentals of spatial analysis change very little over time. A good reminder of this can be seen in the work of John Snow in Victorian London since he used what we would now consider spatial analysis techniques (among others) to help identify the source of the infamous cholera outbreak of 1854. Fundamentally, no matter what techniques or software we use, spatial analysis can be thought of as the process of creating or extracting new *information* from existing spatial *data*.

We will now illustrate the 'what and how' of spatial analysis methods by using four different examples here. In the first example, we look at how many people live within a distance of a specific location using a simple straight-line (Euclidean) distance measure. In the second example, we answer the question of 'what is nearby?' by taking the same location and looking at the issue from the perspective of travel time by public transit. In the third example, we turn to look at the issue of connectivity by exploring the issue of how connected places are. For this, we refer to some recent work on 'megaregions' in the United States since it provides a good example of testing Tobler's First Law with real-world data. This is a good example of the way that spatial analysis can help us move from what at the outset may appear to be a mess of data towards more structured knowledge. Following these examples, the final part of this section explains in more detail the most common spatial analysis techniques used in contemporary GIS packages.

Example 1: how many people live 'near' Manchester Airport?

In this example, we have two kinds of geographic data. The first is a point, which represents the location of Manchester Airport's control tower. The other kind of data is a polygon layer, which contains small area population counts. The basic spatial analysis question here is 'how many people live within 5 km of Manchester Airport'? We use the 5 km distance since it has been shown to be a kind of critical cut-off in terms of noise pollution (Wolfe et al., 2014) and therefore represents a realistic use case for this kind of spatial analysis. The answer to this question can then help us understand how many people might be affected if, for example, aircraft movements were increased or if more night flights were scheduled.

As we can see in Figure 7.3, the area selected is not perfectly circular. This is due to the fact that the polygon layer that contains the population data is comprised of irregularly shaped polygons. This is a very common feature of administrative geographies across the world, in that they do not often allow us to ask spatial questions with the degree of precision we might like. Nonetheless, we have identified all census Output Areas here that are partly or wholly within 5 km of Manchester Airport. This returns a total population of just under 160,000 based on the results of the 2011 Census and helps answer the question of how many people live 'near' Manchester Airport. If we select only those Output Areas completely within the 5 km buffer, the population count is just under 125,000. This area is also shown in Figure 7.3.

Figure 7.3   *Population living in Output Areas 'within' 5 km of Manchester Airport*

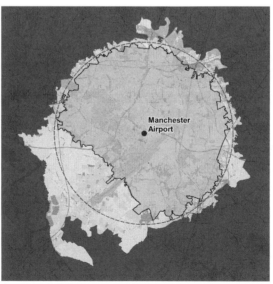

Example 2: how many people live within 30 minutes of Manchester Airport?

As we have noted above, another important kind of 'nearness' is temporal rather than spatial proximity. Straight-line (or Euclidean) distance is important for issues like noise pollution, but more important for things like accessibility and employment opportunities is how long it takes to get somewhere. Given the fact that nearly 20,000 people work at Manchester Airport, it is of course important that they can access the site easily, so in this example we ask the question of how many people live within 30 minutes of Manchester Airport by public transport. This will help give us some idea of the range of employees who might realistically be able to access jobs on site using buses, trams and trains. Using a notional arrival time of 9 am on a weekday, we have identified all areas within 30 minutes of Manchester Airport by public transport. In this case, we can see that 45,000 people live within this area. At different times of the day, of course, this figure will vary, owing to the level of traffic congestion and the availability of public transport.

In Figure 7.4, we can see that the results of this analysis produce a very different geography to the previous example – a much smaller geographic area. Here, the spatial pattern is driven by the connectivity of the underlying road, rail and tram network since this dictates whether areas are within the specified time zone. Perhaps unsurprisingly, the area is not very large in geographic terms since traffic congestion is often a major problem in and around international airports such as Manchester. Nonetheless, this use case provides another good example of the kinds of fundamental spatial analysis questions we need to answer in planning and the built environment. Further examples of network analysis questions such as this are provided in Chapter 8, so here we simply wish to emphasise again the extent to which the question of how 'near' one place is to another can depend on how

Figure 7.4   *Area within 30 minutes of Manchester Airport by public transport*

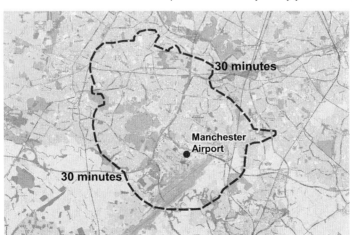

nearness is conceived of in the first place. When we are thinking of 'location', then, we need to think not just in terms of straight-line distance, but also network distance.

Example 3: how connected are the towns and cities of the United States?

The examples of how many people live within a set distance of a place, or a set time, come up again and again in spatial analysis and are presented above as foundational examples. If we wish to take the Tobler question one step further, however, we could ask not simply how many people live near a certain location, but also how connected they are. This requires some additional complexity since we must first determine how to measure 'connectedness'. A good example of this comes from work on the 'Megaregions' of the United States by Nelson and Rae (2016). If we accept the idea that 'everywhere is connected to everywhere else, but near things are more related than distant things' then we might justifiably ask how we could measure 'degree of connectedness'.

The question of the 'natural' economic geography of the United States has been approached from several different perspectives in the past, but Nelson and Rae sought in their work to empirically assess the extent to which small areas in the Lower 48 States were connected or disconnected from each other from an economic geography point of view. If, as Tobler proposed, near places are more connected than distant places, then we might expect higher commuter flows between proximate locations, and this is what Nelson and Rae examined.

Using a complex network partitioning algorithm, they analysed the commute patterns of 130 million US commuters in order to identify the extent to which individual areas of the United States were connected internally. This was done with reference only to the total commute volume between locations and not the distance between them; in effect, it was a test case for Tobler's First Law. At first, this simply involved looking at the census tract to census tract commute flows between places, as in Figure 7.5, but this in itself is difficult to interpret, so it requires some further analysis. The results, as shown in Figure 7.6, demonstrate that the economic geography of the United States can actually be expressed in a series of 'Megaregions' which are internally well connected from a functional economic point of view, but less well connected with areas further away.

This map (Figure 7.6) represents regions which have a very high degree of internal connectivity but a low degree of connectivity with neighbouring regions. It is, then, a kind of representation of how the economic geography of the United States works in practice, in contrast to the underlying geography of states, counties and other smaller geographic units. Connectedness, in this sense, is measured by a value known as network 'modularity', which ranges between 0 (not well connected) and 1 (very well connected). In the case of the US megaregions in Figure 7.6, the modularity score was 0.95, suggesting a very well connected series of megaregions. In effect, then, this confirms the general rule enshrined in Tobler's First Law, even if there are some exceptions (e.g. extra long-distance commutes).

Figure 7.5   *Tract to tract commuting flows in the United States*

Figure 7.6   *'Megaregions' derived from tract to tract commute connections*

Some common spatial analysis operations

The examples in the previous section provide an initial overview of how spatial analysis is more than simply mapping data. It is, as we have said, a way of deriving new information from existing spatial data. In practice, there are many different kinds of spatial analysis, so here we present some of the most useful and common ones found in software packages such as ArcGIS, MapInfo and QGIS, in addition to some explanation of what they do and when they might be useful. We present these here owing to their relevance to planning and the built environment.

Select by Location

One of the most powerful tools in any GIS analyst's toolbox is the ability to query data geographically. This is a type of analysis uniquely suited to GIS software and allows us to answer the all-important 'what is nearby?' question that dominates spatial analysis. Take, for example, the question of how many buildings are near a major road. This might be relevant if the road was being widened, for example. In the example in Figure 7.7, we have shown a section of Grand Avenue in Chicago and all buildings within 500 m of it. Using a 'Select by Location' operation in ArcGIS, we have identified all buildings in Chicago which are within 500 m of Grand Avenue. The results show that there are just over 23,000 buildings in this zone, an extract of which you can see in Figure 7.7.

Understanding the Select by Location operation is a really fundamental part of mastering the principles of spatial analysis. We have used it here to identify all polygons (in this case buildings) that are within a specified distance of another geometry class (in this case a road). To put it another way, we have simply asked the GIS to find all polygons within 500 m of a polyline. We could do the same thing using any combination of points and polygons, in addition

Figure 7.7   *Buildings within 500 m of Grand Avenue in Chicago, Illinois*

Figure 7.8 *Buildings within 1000 m of the United Center*

to some distance criteria. In the example in Figure 7.8, we have selected the building polygon for Chicago's United Center and then performed the Select by Location operation to identify all buildings within 1000 m of it.

Buffers

Related to the Select by Location query in spatial analysis is the creation of buffers. This allows us to create new polygons at a set distance around a particular feature, to help identify an area of interest. For example, if we wanted to create a permanent geographic layer which covers the area 500 m on either side of Chicago's Grand Avenue, we could create a single buffer polygon to this effect. This can be done simply and quickly in any modern GIS package; the results of which are shown in Figure 7.9 below.

Figure 7.9 *500 m buffer along Grand Avenue in Chicago*

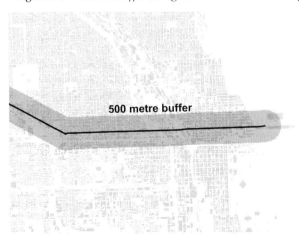

Figure 7.10   *500 m Grand Avenue buffer, with public parks shown*

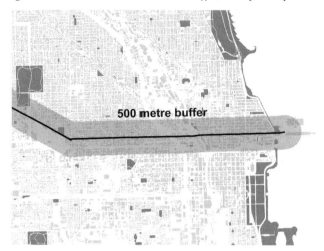

Whereas Select by Location is a useful tool for querying data and obtaining almost instant spatial results, creating a buffer around a feature is more akin to creating a permanent 'area of interest' which we can then use for further analysis. For example, we might also be interested to see how many public parks are within the 500 m buffer area, as shown below in Figure 7.10.

The examples demonstrate simple ways in which the use of spatial analysis can help us create new information from existing spatial data based on the concept of 'what's nearby'. This is perhaps the most common kind of GIS question, but of course there are many more. One of the more important ones relates to the question of spatial distributions and densities, as we explain in the next section.

Spatial aggregation

One of the most useful features of a geographic information system is the ability to summarise data spatially. Just as in the example of US commuter flows in 'Example 3: how connected are the towns and cities of the United States?', it is often the case that the patterns we see in spatial data through a visual approach may not be an accurate depiction of any underlying geographic patterns. A good example of this is when we have many thousands of individual points in a small area. This is often the case in residential real estate analysis where there can be several thousand points in close proximity. In Figure 7.11, we have plotted a sample of more than 4000 residential real estate transactions in London between 2010 and 2015, in addition to the geography of the underlying London Boroughs. What we can discern from this is rather limited. For example, we can tell that there is a degree of clustering in central London and fewer transactions in some outer Boroughs. But it is very difficult to say much more than this without performing some further spatial analysis. This is where the basic 'point-in-polygon' type analysis comes into play.

In the second map (Figure 7.12), we have produced a choropleth map showing the total number of transactions in each Borough. The Boroughs cover different geographic areas and we cannot discern from the map the number of

Figure 7.11   *Sample of residential real estate transactions in London, 2010–2015*

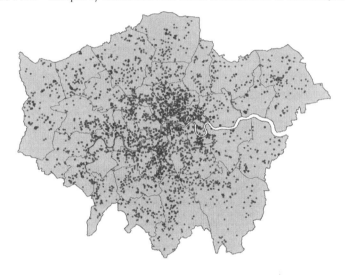

Figure 7.12   *Summary of residential real estate transactions in London, 2010–2015*

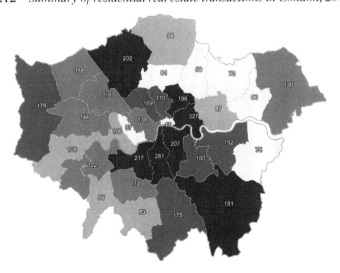

houses in each area, but with this approach it is possible to definitively say how many sales there have been in each area, and to look for a pattern. Again, this is a good example of how spatial analysis operations enable us to derive new information from existing data.

We have sought here to provide an introduction to spatial analysis and some example use cases. The next chapter looks at some more complex examples in relation to network analysis and how they can be solved using a GIS approach. The important point here is that readers understand the basic principle that spatial analysis is a powerful tool for answering geographic questions and deriving new information from existing data. Once again, however, we urge caution. Spatial analysis can be immensely powerful, but it is not definitive. Human decision making will always have a role to play in setting parameters, interpreting results and deciding what the questions are in the first place. In the Chicago example using a buffer function, this might relate to how we set distance thresholds and in the London example it might relate to the scale at which we aggregate data. Put simply, the world we seek to model is complex and nuanced, so we should always seek to acknowledge this complexity in our work.

A note on distance and connection

At the beginning of the chapter, we invoked Tobler's 'First Law of Geography'. This was both necessary and appropriate, but of course it is also something of a simplification. If 'near things' really are more related than 'distant things', an important question is 'what do we mean by near'? In this case, it is clear that Tobler was referring to geographic proximity and that, in general, spatially proximate things are more related than distant things. But, of course, distance can be measured in different ways. For example, Chapter 8 looks at distance from the perspective of networks, whereas here we mainly focused on straight-line distance. Both of these have their place in spatial analysis, but we must also acknowledge that there are some important exceptions and complications in relation to Tobler's First Law. 'Nearness' is a social as well as a physical concept, and to demonstrate this a famous example from São Paulo comes to mind.

In 2007, Brazilian photographer Tuca Vieira took an aerial photo from a helicopter of the stark contrast between rich and poor areas of São Paulo. The photo (Figure 7.13) shows the favela of Paraisópolis on the left, right next to the affluent Morumbi neighbourhood over the wall. This image is now world-famous and has inspired debates on poverty. It is seen to symbolise the extreme inequalities that exist in many world cities, yet it is also a powerful example of when Tobler's First Law is, perhaps, less appropriate. Here we see two neighbourhoods separated only by a wall and a narrow road; yet in design, scale, wealth and power they are so markedly different. One is apparently overcrowded, informal and poorly planned while the other appears opulent, well landscaped and immaculately presented. These areas

Figure 7.13 *Paraisópolis (left) and Morumbi, São Paulo*

São Paulo, Brazil, 2005. The Paraisópolis favela borders the affluent district of Morumbi in São Paulo, Brazil (Photo: Tuca Vieira)

are near in physical distance, but in every other way they would appear to be very distant. Such examples can be found in cities across the world, and serve as a powerful reminder that spatial proximity is not always a sign of connectedness.

As an exception to Tobler's First Law, then, this may be the prototypical case. Yet it is so powerful precisely because the First Law is most often true. The fact that we see such differences cheek-by-jowl is not the norm and this is why it surprises us here. In the case of Paraisópolis and Morumbi, we could reasonably assume from the photographic evidence that they are not actually very 'near' each other, despite their geographic proximity. We include this image here for two reasons. The first is that it highlights the fact that any 'laws' postulated are bound to be broken, particularly when they are about the social world. The second reason we included this image is that this is a book about GIS for planning and the built environment, and it is entirely possible that exceptions to Tobler's First Law will be relevant to readers, particularly in densely populated urban areas.

Conclusion

In this chapter, we explored the concept of geographic space, discussed the 'First Law of Geography' and provided some examples of spatial analysis methods. These methods can help us understand our world more deeply and help us derive new information from underlying spatial data. This is at the heart of what spatial analysis does and why it is so powerful. In planning and the built environment, however, we must also remember that spatial analysis does not answer the question of why things happen where they do. But, as we have shown, without spatial analysis, the fundamental questions relating to location would be much more difficult to answer in the first place.

There are many fine texts dedicated to the understanding and explanation of spatial analysis (e.g. Longley et al., 2015; de Smith et al., 2018), and for further details on methods and techniques we recommend readers explore these. For now, we hope that we have demonstrated that 'spatial is special', and that by taking a geographic approach to analysis it really is possible to understand the world in new ways.

Chapter 8

Network Problems and How to Solve Them

Introduction

> The day when we can move with no cost in time or effort from one place to another (i.e. a world of 'magic carpets') is the day when can say that the city is dead.
>
> (Storper and Scott, 2016, p. 1130)

So far in this book we have looked at the way that GIS can be used to analyse and solve spatial problems. This has, by and large, meant accepting that spatial relations are primarily and logically based on the idea of distance and proximity. As discussed in Chapter 7, Tobler's First Law is the clearest and most famous embodiment of this idea; of the value of proximity measures that are based on Euclidean geometry (or spherical projections of Euclidean space) in the formulation and solution of 'real-world' problems.

But sometimes Euclidean geometry, and the idea of 'straight-line' distance, is a rather limiting concept. It is often a somewhat poor representation of real-world spatial systems. By contrast, the idea of *network space* is commonly used to model complex spatial systems which emphasise the role of *topology* over distance-based measures of *proximity*. Simply put, within network space we are interested in *how connected* things are rather than merely *how near* they are. In such thinking, connections can vary in their quality or capacity (e.g. roads have different allowable or achievable speeds; or social networks can be stronger or weaker). The capacity for such connections to vary means that the *topological space* implied by a network may be quite different to that of Euclidean space. Things that are far away in terms of distance may actually be very well connected (e.g. two distant cities that enjoy a frequent direct air service).

It should already be clear that network models offer significant potential for planners interested in constructing more accurate representations of real-world systems, especially those that depend on interactions between places and things. For these reasons, network models find significant use in the fields of transport planning and retail planning, as well as within industries such as transport services or logistics management where an understanding of the 'real' costs of mobility enables a significant competitive advantage. Other fields that have traditionally used, and continue to use, the benefits of network analysis include

129

emergency service planning, education planning (for problems such as finding the best sites for new educational facilities) and housing markets analysis.

Network models also provide the computational heart of consumer facing technologies such as satnavs and 'find my nearest' locational services. Services such as Google Maps and Bing Maps have sophisticated routing algorithms that determine the best routes or nearest facilities based on near-real-time estimates of traffic speed. Significant investments in fixed-sensor and crowdsourced data collection on traffic speeds and public transport networks have enabled sophisticated global infrastructures to be developed that allow network analysis to be based on accurate measurements of the quality of transport links at any given point in time. These are enabling the deployment of real-time informatics approaches to logistics and network management problems.

The applications of network models are various and allow the construction of sophisticated GIS analyses of dynamic processes that account more realistically for *anisotropy* in the real world. Network models have found great favour among transport planners, retail planners, logistics professionals and others who place a premium on accurate modelling of the way people and things move about space.

This chapter will discuss the key concepts involved in network models and analysis, focusing on the system of *nodes* and *links* that are usually employed to represent real-world networks such as those found in transport or telecommunications infrastructure. Three distinct 'classes' of analytical problem are discussed: routeing, accessibility and location-allocation.

Key concepts

Analytically speaking, networks comprise *nodes* and *links* in an integrated topology which can be computationally interrogated. Nodes and links can hold attributes about the nature of those objects and their implications for their behaviour. These may be codified as rules (such as those mandating, permitting or forbidding certain actions by certain classes of agent), restrictions (such as limits or constraints on the capacity of the link or node within the network) or other characteristics such as the cost or time of traversing the link or node.

The ontology of a network might be best understood by reference to a GIS model of a road network, of the type that might be found in a satnav. In such a model, the *links* are representations of roads, while the *nodes* are representations of junctions between roads. Roads vary in important ways, which can be captured using attributes within the base network dataset. The table, or layer, representing the road links may have attributes with information such as the road classification (normally taken as an indication of its hierarchical importance), the speed (e.g. a speed limit or perhaps even information on typically achieved speeds in varying traffic conditions), the capacity of the road and so on. Other attributes in a road network model might include information on other 'costs' associated with traversing that link: road tolls, gradients, vehicle restrictions and so on.

Box 8.1   Making sense of network terminology

Edges, vertices, nodes, arcs…confused? If you are, this is hardly surprising given the number of different terms used to describe the key components of a network. But, by and large, the terms can be used interchangeably. Software products might use different terms, but they are more or less analogous to each other. The following table is a summary of some of the key terms used to refer to the key ingredients of a network model:

Representations of facilities…	*Representations of routes…*
Nodes	Links
Vertices	Edges
Junctions	Arcs
Points	Lines

The roads provide connections between junctions, represented as nodes. Nodes may also hold attributes. In our example, important attributes might be: junction type (e.g. free-flow or signal-controlled), any turn restrictions (e.g. no right turn) or mandates (e.g. 'ahead only'). A representation of a grade separated road layout might also need to include information about nodes where no physical correspondence between links is possible by including attributes on the elevation of the associated road links.

Accessibility

Accessibility, as with a handful of other concepts such as density, is central to the work of planners. Indeed, 'accessibility analysis can be said to be one of the fundamental analyses of GIS' (Dahlgren, 2008, p. 16). Variation in accessibility contributes in very great part to the anisotropic nature of the built environment. With few exceptions, civilisations have emerged not on featureless plains, but in topographies characterised by natural and physical barriers to mobility. To these barriers must be added the countless human-made impediments and enablers of the free movement of people: walls, private land and choked transport arteries all impose real costs (if not total barriers) on movement, and thus can lessen the accessibility to important services or markets for certain populations but not others. On the other hand, infrastructure like bridges, tunnels, air services, fibre-optic links and satellite telecommunications serve to overcome the tyranny of distance and to leap physical barriers, in the process reducing the real costs of connecting selected places or populations with one another, improving accessibility in the process.

   Many factors govern accessibility. It is a broad concept, informed in part by spatial scale. At the level of individual streets and buildings, we know that accessibility can be entirely determined, and mitigated, by design details such as the configuration of pavements, the height of kerbs, the width of corridors and the design or availability of stairs, elevators and doors. At the other extreme, global accessibility may be measured in terms of the capacity in gigabits per second of key digital communications links, the availability and frequency of scheduled air services or by political arrangements permitting cross-border transit of people and goods. Key technologies can at a stroke overcome the impossibilities of distance or inhospitable terrain or regimes, and history is full of examples where new networks have transformed accessibility overnight, redrawing the map of trade or political relations in the process. Some examples of technologies that have transformed accessibility in history are set out in Table 8.1. In each case, it is clear that any map of accessibility that is based solely on distance runs the risk of becoming redundant at a stroke, to be replaced by one favouring the assimilation of new *network connections*. What is also clear from the table is that network analysis concepts, and their relationship to the concept of accessibility, are not solely related to fixed transportation infrastructure, but can relate to more ephemeral concepts such as timetables, services and social relations.

Accessibility is both a disaggregate and an aggregate concept. The accessibility of one singular facility to a specific individual can be proxied by a number of measures, which are dependent on network attributes (such as network distance, time, cost or connectedness). A low cost link between facility and user, for example, would imply a high level of accessibility, and vice versa. Thus, disaggregate accessibility can be measured for identifiable facilities and individuals. But it is also possible to measure the overall, *aggregate*, level of accessibility to a facility (or class of facilities) within a broader spatial system. Examples abound in worlds of retail analysis and transport planning, among others. The total proportion of a city's addresses that are within a five-minute walk of a public transport stop or station might be a simple aggregate measure of the accessibility of public transport. The average drive time for a city's residents to their nearest supermarket, perhaps weighted in some way such as by income, might be the kind of aggregate accessibility metric that a retail strategist looking for competitive advantage in store location might employ.

Accessibility measures, especially of the aggregate kind, are essential ingredients for location-allocation problems, which seek to answer sophisticated questions related to the optimal location of candidate facilities with respect to a spatial dispersed and heterogeneous demand population.

Algorithms and heuristics

All network analyses depend on the basic idea of calculating the path of least cost within a network. In theory, this involves evaluating the aggregate cost of every possible route between a given origin and destination, and selecting the route with the lowest cost. In practice, this is not feasible because of the unmanageably huge number of permutations normally yielded by networks. To illustrate this, we can take the case of a relatively simple grid-iron road network with eight north–south streets and six east–west streets (as in Figure 8.1).

Figure 8.1 *Illustration of simplified grid-iron road network*

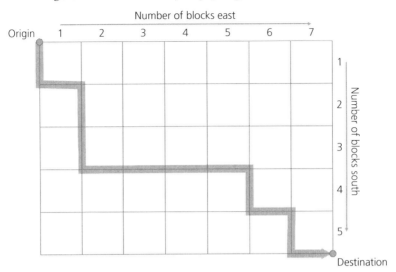

In this simplified example, in which all block distances and associated costs are equal, there are 792 possible routes from origin to destination. The grey line denotes one of those 792 possible routes. No backtracking (moving away from the destination) or U-turns are allowed; if they were, the number of possible permutations would increase greatly.

Assuming that no backtracking or U-turns are allowed (i.e. the vehicle must always be moving closer to its destination), then evaluating this problem would involve calculating the cost of traversing $\frac{12!}{7!5!} = 792$ possible paths through the network. The implications for computing power can be readily appreciated if we take the number of road links in Great Britain as an example. The freely downloadable OS OpenRoads network dataset, which maps the public highway network in England, Scotland and Wales, contains over 3.1 million traversable links and more than 2.6 million individual nodes. For most purposes, it is not possible to comprehensively evaluate every possible routing permutation on such a network. For this reason, network analysis tools commonly turn to heuristic approaches, employing computer algorithms, to efficiently calculate optimal routes between given origins and destinations.

The basis for most analytic approaches is Dijkstra's (1959) 'single-source shortest-path' algorithm. This is an algorithm which takes a starting point node, evaluates the cost to all immediately connected nodes and iterates this process until it has found a least-cost path to a destination. A precise explanation of how Dijkstra's algorithm works is beyond the scope of this book, but interested readers will find an accessible explanation on the ESRI website (see ESRI, n.d.). The key point about this algorithm is that it is guaranteed to find the least-cost path without necessarily having to evaluate every possible route permutation in the network. Computationally, there have been various advances on this algorithm, including those that optimise for processing speed, but the basic logical behaviour that the algorithm seeks to operationalise

Table 8.1 *Examples of network technologies and their impacts on accessibility*

Era	Technology	Key network attributes	Impact on accessibility	Broader impacts
1860s	Suez Canal	New link	Reduced sailing distances by 7000 km; reduced sailing times	Opened up global markets in the East. Reduced price of oil from the Middle East to US and other Western markets
1870s	Metropolitan railway from London to Middlesex	New links; increased speed and capacity of existing transport links/corridors	Reduced travel time to central London from several hours to 30 minutes	Suburbanisation of outer London; underpinned new speculative housebuilding activity; consolidated role of existing centre (London)
1900s	RMS *Mauretania* ocean liner	Increased speed and capacity of existing transport links/corridors	Holder of record for fastest transatlantic sea crossing for two decades; world's largest ship at time of completion	Reduced costs of intercontinental travel; stimulated competition for larger and faster ocean liners
1950s	Intercontinental ballistic missiles	Increased speed and range of existing rocket-based technologies	Deliver nuclear weapons across the globe within 30 minutes	Global nuclear strategy, geopolitical relations, arms race
1960s–2010s	Boeing 747 jet airliner	Increased capacity and range of existing 'link' (air corridors)	Lower costs of air travel	Globalisation of tourism, labour mobility and trade

1970s	ARPAnet/Internet global digital telecommunications network	New links, increased capacity of links	Lower costs and increase reliability of data transmissions	Global technological markets and innovation, impact on service delivery, social relations, commerce
2000s	Øresund bridge-tunnel	Replacement link (replaces road/rail ferry); new link (data)	Reduce cross-border travel time between Malmö (Sweden) and Copenhagen (Denmark). Provide direct rail, road and data links between Scandinavia and continental Europe	Increased cross-border commuting, trade, economic production (GDP) in Sweden and Denmark
2010s	Verizon Chicago–New York data link	New link, increased speed	Reduced round-trip data transmission speeds between Chicago and New York by 0.5 ms to <15 ms (light would take 13.3 ms)	Increased electronic trading volumes; enhanced competitiveness of High-Frequency Trading companies

remains pertinent. Variants of Dijkstra's algorithm are the basis for the range of network analysis tools provided in ArcGIS Network Analyst extension; there are also tools available for other proprietary GIS, including RouteFinder for MapInfo Professional, and rapidly developing open source tools which implement Dijkstra's algorithm such as the RoadGraph plugin for QGIS.

Data

As far as the typical analyst seeking to leverage the potential of networks in their work is concerned, the key constraint on, or determinant of, their likely success lies in the quality and cost of available data.

Network models place great demands on data and on processing capacity. In particular, there is a need to use highly structured data on the base network, and most network modelling problems place a great premium on assembling and structuring appropriate data. Particular care must be taken to assemble datasets that have topological integrity, the appropriate attributes and are complete. The specific import of each of these is now discussed briefly.

Topological integrity – Within a network model, how the features are connected with one another is of paramount importance. If there is no connection between two features, then the analysis tools within the GIS will not be able to find a legitimate path or solution. Therefore, nodes that are connected by links need to be exactly spatially coincident if there is an actual topological connection between them that needs to be modelled (Figure 8.2). Furthermore, the actual nature of the connection needs to be systematically recorded within the model. Spatial coincidence may not necessarily imply an actual connection: on a motorway flyover, the overpass will be spatially coincident with the

Figure 8.2   *The importance of topological integrity in network datasets*

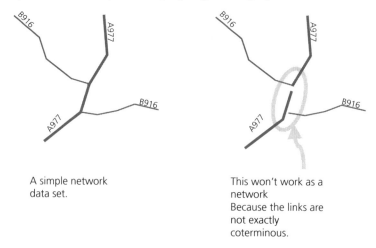

A simple network data set.

This won't work as a network Because the links are not exactly coterminous.

underpass, but there is no actual possible correspondence between the two roads. Accuracy is key: nodes and links must be very accurately aligned. (It should be noted that network analysis tools may allow the specification of an acceptable spatial tolerance within which nearby nodes will be considered coincident, and this can be used to overcome some of the problems associated with inaccurate data.)

Attributes – In the absence of any relevant attributes about the links and nodes comprising a network dataset, the only possible analyses are those that proceed on the basis of *network distance*. By applying a global assumption about speed (e.g. an average driving or walking speed), this can be converted into time. If the network dataset contains attributes that allow a differentiated picture of the specific costs of traversing network links to be built up, it is clear that more sophisticated analyses can be undertaken that will be a better reflection of *anisotropy* (i.e. directionality) in the 'real world'. Assembling an appropriate set of attributes is an important element of the task of constructing a network dataset. It is probably more in the attributes than in the underlying geometry of a network dataset that the most 'value' is found in terms of reflecting the work that has gone into creating it – commercial providers of road network datasets, such as HERE or TomTom, compete with each other on the quality and breadth of their attribute data, including time variant measures of average speeds, accurate depictions of the road hierarchy and detailed information on route capacity and restrictions (e.g. prohibitions for certain classes of vehicles). These rich attributes allow increasingly sophisticated analyses to be built up, measuring differences in accessibility for different times of the day, under different network loading conditions and for different types of vehicle.

Coverage and completeness – For a network analysis to provide satisfactory and useful results, it depends on having a sufficient level of coverage and completeness in the basic network model for the analysis's scale and purpose. In terms of coverage, the model must not omit important parts of the network (or levels of the network hierarchy) appropriate to the purpose or spatial scale of the analysis. For example, a vehicle routing application that is used to manage long-distance freight logistics might use a base network model comprising just the key links in a country's road network (e.g. motorways and primary routes). If the model does not have detail of local roads this may be of little significance in terms of the usefulness of the overall analysis. In contrast, an analysis of optimal health care facility locations within a city will demand a base network model with coverage of local roads and streets. In both cases, it is important that the network model is complete insofar that all links of the appropriate type are included for the area of interest. For network analysis, this usually means including links within the network model that may be outside the area of interest. Optimal routes may involve traversing links that go outside of an administrative zone: for example, an accurate city-based analysis of retail accessibility might depend on incorporating links that go outside the city's boundary. This problem applies equally

Figure 8.3   *Vehicle routing solutions involving adjacent territories*

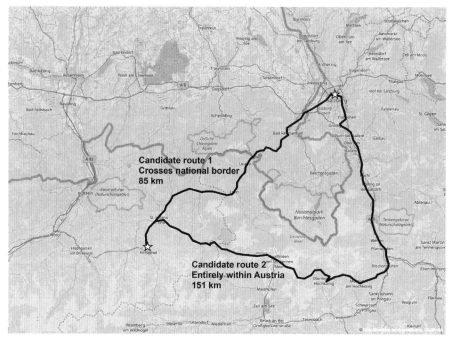

Source: background map from © OpenStreetMap contributors (https://www.openstreetmap.org/copyright)

to international routeing problems. To illustrate, we can take the example of the fastest road journey between the Tirol region and the city of Salzburg in Austria (Figure 8.3). This route involves a short section traversing Bavaria, in Germany. A national network model of Austria would therefore deliver unrealistic results if it did not incorporate information on links and nodes within adjacent territories.

This map shows three candidate driving routes between the Tirol and Salzburg in Austria. All three routes involve traversing part of Germany, demonstrating the importance of incorporating information from adjacent areas.

The basic options available to analysts are three-fold: use free data, construct a bespoke dataset or buy a commercial dataset. Freely available data, either as a network-ready dataset or as a basis for constructing a bespoke network model, is now a serious option. The most important source here is OpenStreetMap (OSM), which has reached a level of coverage that permits its use in a wide range of applications, including free and commercial consumer satellite navigation apps. OSM data can also be used as a basis for constructing bespoke network models by adding custom attributes based on local knowledge. National mapping agencies are increasingly

Figure 8.4   *Extract of OS OpenRoads network dataset, symbolised by road classification*

Contains OS data © Crown copyright and database right 2018

making datasets freely available which can be used for network problems and routing analysis. One such product is the British Ordnance Survey's OS OpenRoads dataset (Figure 8.4). This comes with a range of useful attributes such as the length of links and the classification of road type, which cut down on the amount of intermediate processing that end users need to do. But these 'open' products have their shortcomings. In the case of OS OpenRoads, the most significant omission is in its lack of information on road speeds (whether posted limits or typical actual speeds). Given that road speeds can vary dramatically according to road type, junction design, local circumstances and congestion at different times of the day, it is essential that any analyst wishing to use data such as this invests a bit of time applying some basic assumptions that can help to insert a bit of realism into the resulting model. Free datasets of this sort are unlikely to include information on detailed turn or use restrictions, mandatory traffic movements, tolls and other types of 'cost'.

This means inevitably that, unless fully commercial products are purchased, the use of free datasets will in essence require some sort of bespoke development. But, depending on the application, they may offer the basis for a perfectly adequate model – especially for wider scale (e.g. international, national and regional) applications where the effect of very localised restrictions would only have a very marginal impact on overall travel times. By combining free network data with other datasets, a scheme of travel speed assumptions that is sensitive to different combinations of attributes can be quite quickly built up. Box 8.2 sets out a suggested approach for using OS OpenRoads data with other information such as speed assumptions and spatial data on the extent of built-up areas to sensitise the network model to more realistic travel speeds.

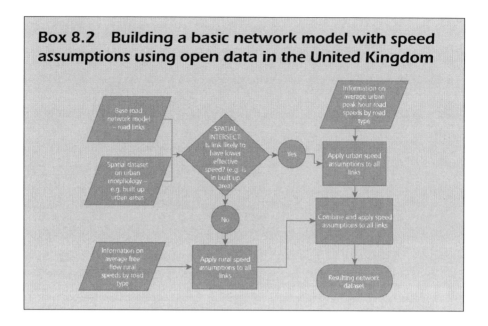

> **Box 8.2   Building a basic network model with speed assumptions using open data in the United Kingdom**

Outputs and applications

This section of the chapter considers the main types of analytical output that can be generated by network analysis, and some examples of their application. These forms of analysis and variants of them can be accomplished by many commercial and open source GIS tools, although arguably the most powerful desktop software for network analysis is ArcGIS's Network Analyst extension (see Box 8.3).

There are probably three basic problems that network analysis helps to solve (Figure 8.5). These are: point-to-point (routeing) problems (including more

Figure 8.5   *Three problem types*

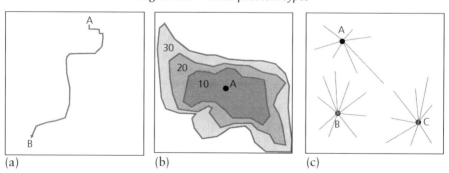

(a) Depicts a classic simple point-to-point routeing problem showing the optimal (e.g. quickest) route from A to B; (b) extends this by solving multiple point-to-point routes for every possible origin to derive an accessibility map showing drive time in minutes to facility A; (c) uses accessibility surfaces for multiple facilities (A, B and C) to determine the optimal allocation of demand points to facilities.

complex logistical problems such as the 'Travelling Salesperson Problem'); accessibility problems, including the generation of drive-time models and 'service areas'; and location-allocation problems that seek to optimise siting decisions. Each is essentially a development of the other, in that all involve the calculation and evaluation of multiple candidate routes between sets of origins and destinations (or the use of a heuristic to sift routes). The location-allocation problem is a logical extension of the accessibility problem in that it considers aggregate accessibility to a range of candidate facilities and evaluates optimum solutions.

Point-to-point routes

The classic routeing problem is at the heart of numerous commercial applications. It is the solution to this problem that enables satellite navigation systems to calculate optimal routes between a given origin and destination, both prior to departure and on-the-fly in response to deviations in the actual route taken or received updates on road conditions. The precise route chosen by the system depends on the attributes programmed into the 'network model' and the parameters chosen by the use. If the network model contains accurate information on average traffic speeds for a particular time of the day, for example, then that would permit the calculation of optimal routes in terms of travel time if that is what the use wished. If the model included topographical information on heights above sea level and the inclines of each road link, then the system would allow a calculation of a route that optimised the number of calories burned by a cyclist.

More complex point-to-point problems arise when the user wishes to evaluate a range of different criteria, or wishes to evaluate routes that involve visiting a multiple number of intermediate stops. A modal choice application in transport planning, for example, might involve evaluating multiple candidate routes between the same origin–destination pair using different constraints (e.g. routes available to car users, bus users, train users and pedestrians) and/or different evaluators (e.g. time, monetary cost, distance, etc.).

Perhaps the most notorious application of the point-to-point problem is the Travelling Salesperson Problem (TSP) which has occupied a central position in the discipline of mathematics since the nineteenth century (Cook, 2014). In the TSP, an optimal route (according to some pre-given evaluation criterion, but usually time) is sought which connects an origin with itself via multiple intermediate stops. The thorny part of the problem comes in that the order that the intermediate stops may be visited can vary: finding the optimal order of stops is part of the problem. This ordering may or may not be subject to further constraints: for example, stops 1–3 must be visited in the morning, but stops 4–10 can be visited at any time.

Although the algorithms that are used within desktop GIS programmes tend to employ heuristics and approximations (rather than an exhaustive calculation of all possibilities), even this complex type of problem is now within the scope of the casual GIS user with his or her low-cost desktop PC and free and

Figure 8.6   *The Travelling Salesperson Problem (TSP)*

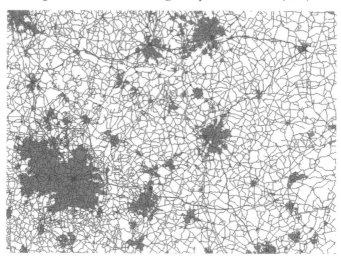

Contains OS data © Crown copyright and database right 2018

open source data. Using a free dataset like OS OpenRoads, ArcGIS's Network Analyst toolkit can be easily set up to solve variants of the TSP by selecting options to allow re-ordering of stops while preserving the origin and destination (Figure 8.6).

Accessibility problems

The general goal in these types of problem is to describe spatial variations in the aggregate accessibility to one or more facilities. The concept of 'accessibility' needs careful definition. It may simply translate to distance, although in network analysis applications this would more normally be a generalised *cost* – for example, taking into account differential travel speeds, or the fuel required to traverse roads of different types. More sophisticated definitions of accessibility might take into account 'psychological' factors such as route complexity (this would be an important element in public transport networks, where minimising changes between bus services might wish to be prioritised).

The subject of the accessibility problem also needs some thought. Often, the individual will be the subject of the analysis; the question will be 'what is accessibility to him or her?'. At other times, however, we might wish to flip the question on its head – 'to whom is this facility accessible?' It is this latter question that has motivated retail analysts and service planners in particular to use network models. Given a real or potential location for a shop or a physical facility (e.g. a hospital), network analysis can answer the question 'how many people live within half-an-hour's drive of this place?'. And furthermore, linking the answer to this with other datasets within GIS allows the logical follow-up question to be addressed: *'what are the characteristics of those people?'*

Figure 8.7   *An isochrone map showing drive time to selected employment centres in the Glasgow city region*

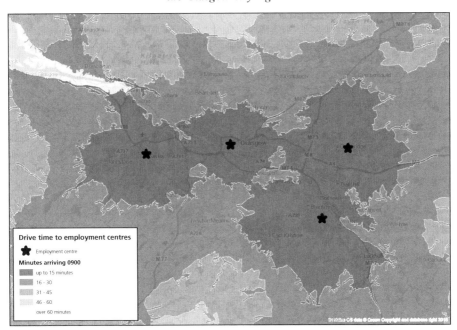

Contains OS data © Crown copyright and database right 2018

The key cartographic device in describing accessibility is the *isochrone*. This is a map where lines describe fronts of equal accessibility (specially, in time – hence 'chrone'). A 15-minute isochrone would be the contour line on a map which traces those locations that are 15 minutes from (or to) a selected facility. The example in Figure 8.7 shows a map with isochrones for 5, 10, 15, 20, 30 and 60 minutes of free-flow drive time (i.e. ignoring the possibility of congestion) to a city centre.

Far from simply allowing retail planners to estimate a captive population's spending power, accessibility problems allow service planners to undertake sophisticated analyses of the aggregate accessibility to a set of multiple facilities. This is particularly useful in highly heterogeneous contexts where the distribution of services or of transport infrastructure is highly variable. Network analysis was used extensively by analysts producing Scotland's new classification of urban and rural areas (Scottish Government, 2014). Their definition of rurality rested not only on settlement size, sparsity, density and other classic 'morphological' characteristics, but also on how accessible settlements were to a range of higher-order settlements and services.

Location-allocation problems

The use of GIS to suggest some sort of optimal configuration of a demand group (population) to a set of services represents, to some extent, the apogee of network analysis. It is also highly computationally intensive. This is because typical problems seek to 'allocate' individual points (e.g. customers or addresses) drawn from very large populations to a set of numerous potential facilities (as in Figure 8.8). The product of the population size and the number of facilities yields often frighteningly large numbers of possible interactions: a relatively modest exercise to allocate 10,000 school pupils to 15 schools would demand the computation of 150,000 optimal routes, for example.

Location-allocation problems are useful not just for allocating populations to facilities, but for appraising the aggregate accessibility of those facilities to that population. This can be helpful in informing decisions as to which facilities to grow, or on which potential sites to target a new facility. Location-allocation would allow a list of potential new facilities to be ranked in terms of their aggregate accessibility to target demand groups.

Extensions to the location-allocation problem allow facilities to be analysed alongside competitors. A retail planner could aim to locate a new store in a place that maximises accessibility for a target demographic while minimising competition from competing stores. The analysis can also incorporate information on the characteristics of the facilities or potential facilities, such as upper bounds on the population that can be serviced (schools might have information on the total number of places available, for example).

Figure 8.8   *Example location-allocation problem, allocating postcodes to supermarkets*

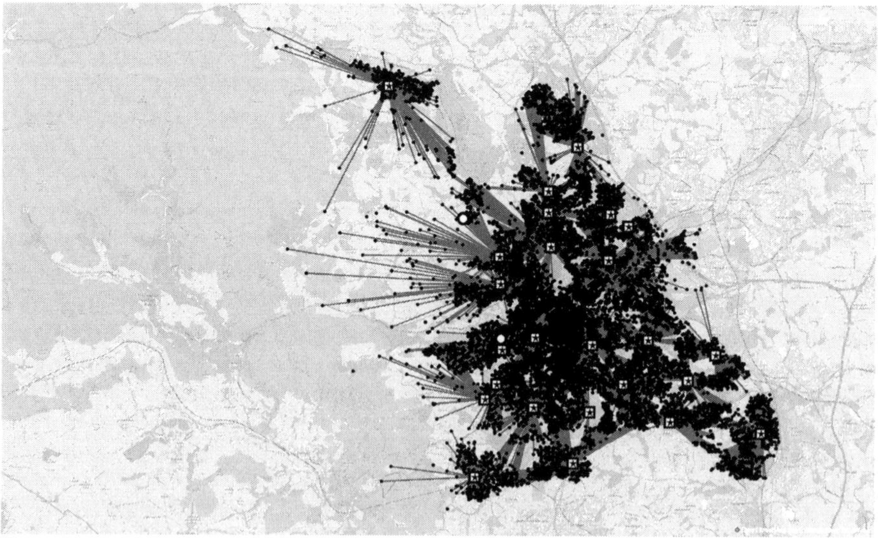

Incidentally, the computation of the solution to a location-allocation problem demands that the GIS produces what is known as an origin–destination cost matrix (OD cost matrix) as a by-product of the analysis. These OD cost matrices can be very useful in their own right, and can permit lots of additional analyses to take place outside of the GIS environment. An OD cost matrix lists every possible pair of origin and destination, and estimates the cost (in whatever units are specified) of making that journey to the criteria set. An analyst could produce a range of OD cost matrices for different transport modes, for example, and subject these to further statistical analysis, perhaps seeking to answer questions such as which origin–destination pairs stand to benefit the most by the construction of a new transport link such as a motorway. This type of analysis is particularly useful in undertaking transport scheme appraisals, and indeed pre-prepared OD cost matrices are usually at the centre of most Land Use Transport Interaction (LUTI) models which are in widespread use by transport planners.

Box 8.3   Performing network analysis in ArcGIS

ArcGIS contains what is probably the most complete set of analysis tools for network analysis within desktop GIS products. While the likes of QGIS and MapInfo Professional have developed useful network analysis tools in recent versions, ESRI's Network Analyst extension for ArcGIS has occupied a mostly unchallenged position in terms of the options it provides to the analyst, and its ability to work with a wide range of network attributes.

Using Network Analyst requires the use of a fully licensed version of the tool. It must be activated from within ArcGIS by selecting the Network Analyst extension from the Customize menu in the ArcGIS application you are using. Additionally, the Network Analyst toolbar should be made visible, again using the Customize menu.

The basic workflow in ArcGIS is as follows.

1. **Build a network dataset.** This provides Network Analysis with the basic network model to work with. The degree of sophistication in the attributes contained within the network dataset determines in large part the types of problems that can be solved. Building a network dataset requires error-free data on the base network (usually a road network). It can be derived from free or commercial sources. Some providers will provide ready-built network models; the cost-conscious user can deploy free sources and add their own attributes (see Box 8.2). Part of the process of building the network dataset involves specifying some of the special attributes that can govern restrictions (e.g. limitations on the availability of a road to certain classes of traffic or at certain times of day), directives (e.g. mandating or prohibiting certain paths through junctions such as right-turns) and adding special information on costs (e.g. tolls). It is also possible to specify a hierarchy of route links which will allow Network Analyst software to take some heuristic 'shortcuts' by

→

$\longrightarrow$

focusing its search for optimal routes on more important links. By doing so, the processing speed is increased, and, while the resulting route may not be fully optimised against the search criteria, it will more closely resemble the routes that would be solved intuitively by humans which will emphasise the use of more important links (e.g. motorways).

2. **Create a new 'problem'.** Network Analysis works using the concept of 'problems', which the user first sets up and then asks the software to 'solve'. Once the skeleton 'problem' is set up in the software, the user loads in details of the points required by the particular problem type. For example, in a route problem, the user will specify 'origin' and 'destination' points. For a service area problem, the user will specify target 'facilities' (e.g. shopping centres). For a location-allocation problem, the user will specify a set of demand points (e.g. service users' home addresses) and a set of candidate facilities (e.g. locations of potential schools).

3. **Set the problem parameters.** It is at this stage that the user would also provide the software with any necessary parameters and criteria to guide the solution to the problem, such as the time intervals required for service areas, whether 'destinations' have to be visited in a particular order, the weights to be applied to different candidate facilities and so on.

4. **Solve the problem!** Finally, satisfied that the problems have been defined correctly, the analyst asks Network Analyst to solve it. The speed of the solution will depend on the complexity of the network, the type of problem, the number of inputs (e.g. origins and destinations), whether or not a hierarchy is used and any special parameters set. A simple point-to-point route may take less than a second to solve, while a location-allocation problem based on hundreds or thousands of demand points and scores of facilities across a city could take hours or days. Once the solution has been found, ArcGIS adds relevant new layers (e.g. the route(s) found, or the candidate facilities chosen) to the Table of Contents, ready for visualisation or further analysis. Useful information is added to the attribute tables of these layers, including the total accumulated network costs incurred (e.g. travel time).

Conclusion

This chapter has introduced the idea of *network analysis* and has argued that it has huge potential for planners interested in modelling real-world problems related to transport, accessibility and the optimal location of facilities and services. By moving beyond the measure of Euclidean distance to a more generalised measure of costs, network analysis tools offer us the means by which we account for the essentially *anisotropic* nature of cities and processes within and between them. The topological space which networks allow us to model privileges *connectedness* over proximity, and is of particular value to us where crude distance may be a poor predictor of actual social or economic relations.

Accessibility, alongside distance, is one of the key concepts used by planners in analysing difference within cities, and in seeking to enact policies in mitigation of its impacts. History is replete with the 'disruptive technologies' of their day, which in many cases have had huge societal impact precisely because they redraw the map of accessibility – be it the metropolitan railway unleashing the possibilities of the suburb; or the jet airliners that literally bring pairs of cities closer together in time; or the optical data links that shave priceless nanoseconds off the speed of electronic trades. These are examples of the importance of network thinking. The places that are on the networks become ever more different from those being left off it. In an uneven world, we need analytical tools that begin to add the required nuance to Tobler's First Law.

Network analysis is computationally intensive. Even today, comprehensive analysis is beyond the capability of most machines, and so the use of *heuristic* algorithms that mimic intuitive approaches to problem solving are adopted. Knowing something about the links in the network helps those heuristics do their job better and faster; thus, just as we look at a paper map and focus on the main highways and motorways to find the 'best' route from A to B, so we can train the computer to do the same. The quality of a network analysis solution is closely related to the quality of the attributes we are able to feed in. Data volumes and processing times can be large; and assembling the basic network datasets can be difficult – while there are some good free and open source possibilities, the most fully featured network datasets remain the preserve of specialist commercial providers who are able to add value to them, for example by incorporating live data on traffic speeds.

Three classes of problems have been reviewed in this chapter, each increasing in sophistication and each logically opening the door for the next. The basic calculation of point-to-point routes, whether for single or for multiple destinations, is shown to be itself a fiendishly complex mathematical puzzle but one which enables a vast array of commercial applications, such as satnav systems or store locator websites. Building from this is the idea of the 'service area', which uses calculation of multiple point-to-point routes to build *isochrone* representations of the bounds of areas that fall within specified network cost parameters – commonly, drive-time maps. And, finally, drawing on the intermediary of the OD cost matrix – a calculation of the costs of travelling from everywhere to everywhere else – we have the location-allocation problem. This allows a way into complex problems that involve massive, heterogeneous and spatially dispersed demand groups or population, and their interrelationships with a set of actual or potential facilities.

With the availability of network analysis tools in desktop GIS packages, including ArcGIS, and the beginnings of promising open source network datasets, there has never been a better time for planners to begin to harness the potential for GIS to far better understand the spatially unevenness of cities.

Chapter 9

Decision Making Using GIS: Bringing It All Together

Introduction

Throughout this book, we have emphasised that GIS is best thought of as a spatial database or representational system of our world. Partnered with the judicious application of relevant spatial analysis techniques, it represents a powerful resource for discovering and asking questions about geographic patterns and relationships on a wide range of social, environmental and economic issues that are of interest to planners and public policy makers.

But GIS is a tool that requires careful and sensitive deployment. It is best seen alongside all the other tools that might exist within the planner's broad toolkit – including skills in listening, political awareness, influencing, analysis, community engagement, co-production, strategy and policy making, and others. Using GIS can certainly help to change the world, but it cannot do the job alone! Along the way, and frequently, difficult decisions will need to be made.

GIS does not make those decisions, and even if it could, it should not be relied on in isolation. GIS can give us some insights to issues and answers to questions, but it does not provide a comprehensive survey of the scene. It does not tell us what questions to ask, nor does it help us to frame our analysis.

So GIS and the spatial analytical concepts and techniques that underpin the technology are simply tools to be deployed alongside other tools to help understand spatial issues and solve specific spatial problems. Using GIS does not automatically lead to greater understanding – rather, the onus is on how we use the insights that GIS permits us to obtain in an intelligent way; and this demands that we understand the distinction between data and information on the one hand and knowledge and wisdom on the other. GIS does solve problems, but only the very specific computational tasks we set up for it. It does not solve the wider problems that matter: it does not, even in the hands of a skilled analyst, automatically solve society's grand challenges or make the world a better place despite the grandiose claims made by software vendors and some advocacy communities. Yes, without doubt, GIS can *help* us to do all those things. In Chapter 4, we discussed a formal conceptualisation of the relationship between data, information, knowledge and wisdom (DIKW), and how they build together to help us understand the limits and potential of evidence such as that facilitated by GIS and allied technologies.

148

In this chapter, we consider the ways that GIS can be integrated within broader structures and decision-making processes found within society's institutions to help users, organisations and communities understand issues and make plans more effectively. We start with the premise – discussed at length in Chapter 2 – that effective plan-making is not solely a technical exercise in which there are incontestable 'truths' and accepted wisdoms. Good plan-making is a visionary activity, and must confront head-on difficult questions about interests, power (including informational power; see Pickles, 1995), access to resources and the ability to be heard. A more optimistic assessment of contemporary planning would see it lying at the intersection of positivism and interpretivism, occupying a pragmatic middle ground which values evidence of a range of different types. We think GIS is above all a pragmatic technology.

In the 1990s, a time when GIS was becoming widely diffused among the planning profession and allied spatial professions, many academic observers were quick to point to what they saw as GIS's role in reasserting the positivist traditions of the past – in which 'scientific' truths held, the role of the expert was privileged and data-driven solutions to social problems tended to be imposed top-down. This was at a time when such 'empiricism' was under attack from human geographers and social theorists seeking to advance a more normative mode of understanding and policy making, one that was capable of being more attuned to the existence of complexity, bias, power, subjectivity and the agency of citizens and communities. Such critics aligned themselves to a more 'deontological' moral theory of ethics (which focuses on procedural fairness in decision making) in contrast to the alleged 'teleology' of GIS (which elevates the end over the means). As Lake (1993) noted, the widespread adoption of GIS by planners was occurring 'despite, or perhaps even because of, the fact that the positivist assumptions embraced by GIS have long since been jettisoned by academic theorists' (p. 404).

Decision making – a communicative art

From the late 1990s, planning theory and practice were deeply influenced by a 'communicative turn'. Inspired by Jürgen Habermas's theory of communicative rationality, scholars such as Patsy Healey and John Forrester reconceptualised planning as a participatory process which emphasises the role and act of communication, and in which rationality relates not so much to scientific empiricism, but to micro-politics and protagonists' aims. Such pragmatism recognised most of the critiques of rational planning and was aligned clearly with a more postmodern take on planning's purpose, including central questions about what constitutes the 'public interest' (Campbell and Marshall, 2002), and, consequently, how the techniques and technologies of planning allude to or collude with such definitions. This challenged the presupposed role of GIS – to render complex ideas more simple, delineated and measurable. We think this presupposition is wrong, and that GIS has a valuable role to play in the complex and conditional world we inhabit.

For our purposes, we can make the following simplified points. First, GIS and spatial analysis are inescapably empirical, with all the limits that having a reductionist model of the world, however sophisticated and nuanced, implies. This means that, second, the analyst and the user of the analysis have a responsibility to use the technology in a proportionate manner. Third, how the knowledge and wisdom generated by the technology are communicated, shared and used are critical determinants of the effectiveness of decision processes and policy making. And, consequently – our fourth point – the fruits of GIS must sit alongside other forms of knowledge and wisdom, within broader political-institutional, ethical and communicative frameworks that seek above all to make fair and effective policy. GIS's role in this is to produce and use maps that can *demonstrate* and *exemplify* issues, and perhaps persuade people, rather than ride roughshod over more intuitive or experiential forms of knowledge.

We return to some of these points in our concluding remarks to this book in which we set out a short manifesto about how GIS can be better used by planners to make better plans. For the time being, we can posit that the way that GIS is used within different organisational contexts – big public sector institutions, private companies, charities, pressure groups, communities and so on – matters in determining its effectiveness in helping to make good decisions.

Organisational issues

Since the turn of the century, we have witnessed a watershed in the democratisation of access to GIS and spatial data, most notably through open data platforms such as OpenStreetMap (established in 2004) and the open GIS movement which has centred around QGIS since its initial release in 2002. GIS and spatial data are no longer the sole preserve of government or big business. At the same time, information ethics and the ramifications of the ascendancy of often malign forces that are so expertly able to integrate personal datasets to influence behaviour are now very big issues. The evolution of the legal framework for the use of personal data, such as the General Data Protection Regulation (GDPR) in Europe, is of deep relevance to users of GIS. Never before have organisations and individuals alike been able to exploit such an abundance of open data, and never before have they shared openly so much about themselves (consciously or otherwise) through the data harvesting tendencies of smartphone apps and modern computer operating systems. Location is a deeply personal attribute.

Organisations and individuals alike are awash with spatial data. It is a well-travelled trope to say that more than 80% of data used by a typical organisation has some sort of spatial component. It is not without truth. With imagination, it is possible that the figure is even higher now given the centrality of geography to the operation and commercial exploitation of the contemporary Internet. The geotagging of our digital lives, of our very thoughts in the case of social media, has given rise to rich new analytical potential in fields as diverse as sociology and urban studies. Uitermark and Boy's (2017) study of Instagram users demonstrates powerfully how geography and social media are fused together to give effect to new representations of the city.

Organisations seeking to make better strategies or policies are now painfully aware that the key challenge is no longer accessing data, but analysing and making sense of it. Throwing money at software solutions no longer seems wise. In many cases – such as in local governments – the persuasive efforts of software companies mean that the enterprise-wide goal of having GIS on every desk is complete. But despite such open access to analytical power, the strive for effective policy making, implementation and impact remains elusive. Widening access to data and GIS has not automatically solved local government's biggest existential crises. Even absent of the spectre of fiscal austerity that so frames post-crisis local government the world over, it would take a special kind of optimist to imagine that the spatialisation of information has fundamentally transformed the business of government.

Where there have been successes, they have had modest origins. Insights have been generated by a small number of key actors who have effectively brought their insight into the committee or board room and used them to persuade. The organisation has not set out to find the answer to the question – it may not have had the ability to imagine that a question needed answering in the first place – but someone has brought it to them: the answer to a question they did not know existed. The phenomenon of the UK supermarket chain Tesco's Clubcard loyalty scheme is perhaps a good example. Loyalty schemes had been a long-standing marketing tool aimed at protecting and growing sales, used by businesses worldwide for decades. The key insight, not originally anticipated by the board of Tesco, was that it was the *information about customers* and the potential to integrate it with other datasets that were far more valuable. The decision-making support that comes from improved customer insight is what has driven such significant investments in spatial data harvesting and processing as those found in the retail sector.

The importance of context

In their book *Managing Geographic Information Systems*, Obermeyer and Pinto (2007) emphasise the importance of understanding the organisational context when considering whether and how to deploy GIS effectively. As they say,

> Managing GIS remains a two-pronged problem: mastery of the technology it-self and understanding how to manage its effective use within an organization in the context of specific institutional mission in service of a specific clientele.
>
> (p. 3)

This demands a lot of the wider 'human' infrastructure for getting things done within organisations. Organisations or groups that hope to be able to use geographic information need to pay attention to developing the right capacity and capabilities that will allow them to commission, receive and act on the knowledge that GIS helps to generate. For large, cumbersome organisations – such as city planning authorities – this can be a particular challenge. Focusing on the technical issues involved in procuring and deploying a GIS technology solution and spatial data infrastructure across many hundreds or thousands of users may miss part of the point if the managers and decision makers are not sufficiently capable of processing and parsing spatial issues or intelligence on those issues and converting them into meaningful strategies and actions. Equally, framing issues, commissioning research and directing projects that could benefit from geographic insight require a thoughtful commissioning approach. The reason that a course in GIS should be compulsory for every student of urban planning is not the hope that all people employed in the service of communities or the built environment are technically proficient in using the latest release of ArcGIS (for example), but rather that they understand enough about it to appreciate its potential benefits and its limitations. People who are managing teams that hope to benefit from spatial insights need to have a good working understanding of what GIS can and cannot do, along with some basic knowledge of how GIS works in practice. As Obermeyer and Pinto (2007) explain:

> Whether working in an urban planning office, a charity, an emergency rapid-response organization, or some other organization for which geographical information is pertinent and necessary, GIS managers must first understand the technology they are supporting.
>
> (p. 314)

So, effective GIS deployment within the context of organisations needs to grapple with the following:

- The key questions that need to be answered and challenges that need to be overcome in pursuit of that organisation's overall mission rather than its technological goals.
- A realistic appraisal of the external political obstacles to change or implementation of policy, and the relative effort that consequently needs to be paid to overcoming these (even when spatial analysis points to 'obvious' answers).
- The varying extent to which individuals within an organisation or a wider stakeholder community (including residents, developers, market agents, policy makers and so on) actually think about issues spatially, and the consequent weight that they may attach to spatial 'solutions'.

Applications and adoption

As we have noted earlier in this book (especially in Chapter 2 and in examples throughout), GIS has a wide range of applications. While not always life-or-death, these applications have the potential to underpin critical policy making in areas that directly affect citizens' welfare, including the management of the built environment. GIS is used routinely to support decisions around the spatial targeting of resources, such as through the identification of socially deprived or geographically disconnected communities. It is used in the execution of routine but otherwise time-consuming bureaucratic processes such as the management of geographically defined consultation exercises or elections. In both these cases, accuracy matters. The question of how organisations adopt GIS into their decision-making DNA is critical.

Within local government in particular there has been a rapid expansion of the adoption of GIS platforms by local authorities. In the United Kingdom, this is a process that began in earnest in the late 1980s following the publication in 1987 of the Chorley report on *Handling Geographic Information*. Adoption of GIS by local government initially had a rather technical flavour, focusing in the early stages on specialist users and job functions. This increasingly gave way as the technology was opened up to wider groups of users supported by expert teams and enterprise-wide spatial data infrastructures. The development of fast data networks, especially the Internet from the mid-1990s, enabled an enterprise- or sector-wide approach to data sharing and availability. Ongoing increases in data processing power and falls in the costs of processing and data storage have been instrumental in bringing GIS software out of the laboratory and onto the planner's desk. This diffusion, more than 30 years in the making, is now mature; and, yet the strategic capacity to make effective use of spatial insights in local government has arguably not kept pace with the technological advances.

Other functions to which public sector organisations routinely apply GIS techniques include policy and plan-making, especially in terms of incorporating specialist analyses of transport accessibility or the visual or environment impacts of development; locational decision making and development site analysis; cartography; and decision support systems more generally. In each case, GIS produces information that can either inform broader discussion or be used directly as an input to operational decision making. As we have implied earlier in this chapter, when the latter occurs it is important to have a system of checks and balances to ensure that spatial information is appropriately sensitised and placed into context.

Ensuring that GIS is used sensitively and in a way that is appreciative of potential errors in data or analysis is therefore critical. Having methods of sense-checking GIS outputs before they feed into policy or decision making is of vital importance if costly mistakes are to be avoided. Errors in conceptualisation or in the execution of a GIS model, as within any data-driven approach, could lead to significant policy failure or mis-targeting. Even if the analysis is sound, the source data may be inaccurate or used inappropriately. The result would be policies being written or decisions being made on the basis of flawed evidence, or perhaps simply suffering from the optimism biases that can occur when primacy is given to 'scientific' evidence over experience.

Implementation problems

For all these reasons, a dose of 'healthy scepticism' is not only encountered frequently within organisations that use GIS, but should also actually be seen as essential. Understanding the drawbacks and limitations of GIS from the perspective not only of the technical experts, but also of users and policy makers is important. This gives rise to a set of very real implementation problems that might be borne in mind by any person or organisation seeking to use a GIS approach. These problems include:

Cultural issues – Organisational cultures may be resistant to new ways of thinking. They may be hesitant to enact changes in working practices or to adopt new technologies. Rather than seeing such cultures as a barrier, a sensitive manager of GIS technologies would seek to recognise the root-cause issues bound up in them, and to learn from the key constituents (rather than peers) about how they might be overcome. Organisations that treat GIS as a technical specialism, within its own silo, rather than functionally embedded into broader processes may struggle to genuinely integrate spatial thinking into existing business practices.

Skills and training – For all that we may advocate for a democratisation of GIS, the software remains unavoidably complex in use. Even as impressive efforts have been made to open up even complex toolkits such as network analysis to web users (e.g. using ArcGIS Online), the underlying principles of spatial analysis and the heavy demands on data mean that even if access to GIS software and data is becoming much more open, access to the skills required to effectively operate the software and get it to answer the right questions remain at a premium. Universities have some culpability here. GIS courses sometimes tend to focus on step-by-step instructions on how to operate particular software products, which might change unrecognisably at the turn of a version number, rather than on the core concepts that unite all GIS regardless of the specific details of their operation. Furthermore, the conceptual richness that might be offered in university-level GIS training will sometimes be abstract and decontextualised – perhaps based on mathematical first principles rather than starting with the substantive problem and adopting a pragmatic, applied approach. Successful GIS use requires investment in good GIS training and people.

Software and deployment costs – These are becoming less of a barrier than they once were. Open software like QGIS has shaken up the market considerably. As noted, it is also increasingly possible to use online resources like ArcGIS Online, which will provide generous trial functionality and where the pricing model for more advanced use will be on a pay-as-you-go basis reducing the risks of upfront investment. But irrespective of whether an organisation chooses a proprietary or open model, it is in the deployment and supporting infrastructure that the real costs will be felt. A decentralised model of GIS deployment within an organisation – where the software is available to a large number of users – comes with the added challenge of managing data resources. Datasets, especially those obtained commercially, are often subject to very stringent licence restrictions. At the very least, best practice demands that GIS managers adopt a rigorous system of version control over data and keep up-to-date, accurate and reliable metadata

(data about the data). This is difficult to achieve in a decentralised context unless attention is given to working practices, training and having a fast and effective IT model for serving spatial data. Proprietary GIS and database vendors have a range of software solutions capable of managing and serving spatial data across hundreds or thousands of users – but they can be costly. Free solutions such as PostGIS (an extension to the open source PostgreSQL database management software) may be free but will have significant learning, deployment and support curves that organisations must not underestimate.

Data costs – Inevitably, the ability to do anything useful with a GIS comes down to having access to the right data. Data costs have fallen significantly in recent years, owing to efforts across the globe by governments to extend and deepen access to key mapping and administrative datasets. The costs to governments of doing this have often been offset by protecting access to certain highly profitable datasets. In Great Britain, for example, access to the most detailed spatial mapping data is restricted by onerous licensing agreements and price models as part of the national mapping agency's (Ordnance Survey's) status as a government-owned company. The emergence of crowd-sourced data such as OpenStreetMap has begun to challenge this model. Yet there remains little doubt that businesses and government entities willing and able to pay commercial terms enjoy a competitive advantage through the quality and currency of the data they can acquire. Organisations that are able to augment public data sources with their own data or through integration with other datasets – such as in the way that credit reference agencies link postal, electoral and tax records with consumer spending profiles – can generate significant financial value. Investment in high-quality data sources and the skills and infrastructure to keep them updated are essential to the business model of many firms.

Process issues – The final type of organisational problem we wish to mention relates to the broader structures and processes for decision making that may exist within an organisation. Some organisations make very fleet-of-foot decisions, perhaps based on heuristics, intuition or frequent use of 'test and learn' approaches. Others may have well-established systems of political scrutiny and oversight, or a statutory duty to consult, before new policies can be adopted. Whatever the model for decision making, managers may find it difficult to act on new insights without first understanding the process of decision making in their own organisational context. Obtaining such an understanding may necessitate attention to the methods used to translate findings into a certain format or use a particular type of language. Traditional packs of board papers, for example, may provide little by way of opportunity to showcase more dynamic representations from spatial analysis, such as animated maps, 3D visualisations or even augmented reality (AR) models. To that end, managers may find it necessary to disrupt existing processes to find a way to integrate spatial thinking into an organisation's decision making.

Conceptual challenges

Finally, in terms of adopting GIS within organisations or processes, it is worth briefly reviewing some of the key conceptual issues. These relate mainly to the limits of applying spatial concepts to the substantive problem at hand – or, put simply, not all problems can be easily reduced to a model. Many 'wicked issues' in society have evaded decades of attempts to understand and evidence them beyond doubt – they remain fundamentally contested and the role of space may be equivocal. The long-standing and unresolved debate around the existence of 'area effects' within studies of social outcomes stands as a case in point: are observable spatial patterns merely a representation of other factors, themselves unevenly distributed in space; or do spatial phenomena themselves have a determinate impact on outcomes? Irrespective of where the 'true' answer might lie in these debates, the GIS user must always take care not to claim a kind of spatial privilege on issues where other, non-geographic, factors might be more significant.

A related problem arises when observable spatial patterns mask the inherent complexity of social or economic systems. Spatial autocorrelation may appear to tell a deceptively simple story about the role of geography in determining outcomes, whereas in reality there may be a number of parallel forces at play. Take the example of an observable spatial pattern in secondary school outcomes in a city. Some poorly performing schools may struggle to attract the best teachers as a result of their location in relation to where teachers live (spatial mismatch), while others may languish in the league table as a result of sorting processes arising from parental choice. Schools with similar outcomes may differ in their trajectories – some may be improving, while others decline. A simple cross-sectional spatial analysis may fail to uncover these important distinctions. Although it may be an uncomfortable truth for many with a natural affinity to quantitative geographic methods, it is most certainly the case that there are important social, economic and environmental scenarios in our world to which Tobler's First Law might not apply.

A final impediment to spatial analysis that it is worth discussing briefly is the so-called 'Modifiable Areal Unit Problem', or MAUP. Most succinctly described by Stan Openshaw (1983), the issue is that significant statistical bias can result from the scheme of areal units (or zones) used in calculating aggregate values (such as average incomes, employment rates, densities and so on). Given that a great deal of social sciences generally and planning tasks specifically rely on such geographical aggregations, this is a non-trivial issue. At best, planners and spatial analysts can be aware of its existence and factor it into any interpretation of findings. The problem is particularly pernicious in that a great many of the geographic units we tend to use for aggregate analyses are based on boundaries drawn up for an entirely different purpose to that which we put them. The common usage in planning of postal geography (zones normally devised in the pursuit of operational efficiency of postal deliveries) and electoral geography (which may reflect underlying population density or indeed be subject to deliberate gerrymandering), for example, may be problematic because these can be poor substitutes for the phenomenon being studied. Figure 9.1 provides

Figure 9.1 *The Modifiable Areal Unit Problem (MAUP)*

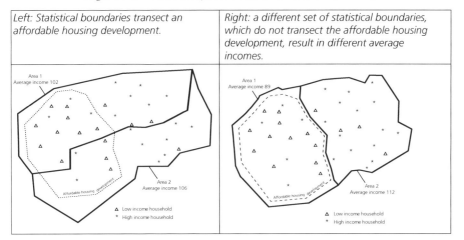

Left: Statistical boundaries transect an affordable housing development.	Right: a different set of statistical boundaries, which do not transect the affordable housing development, result in different average incomes.

a demonstration – it shows that calculations of the average household income for two adjacent areas are dependent on how the boundaries of those areas are drawn. Varying the boundaries yields very different calculations of average income, and therefore different conclusions.

Some technical models for decision making

Bearing in mind all the caveats outlined in the previous section of this chapter, it is clear that GIS offers the planner and policy maker a significant number of technical possibilities to aid decision making. Indeed, there have been notable efforts within the development of spatial analysis and GIS software environments to generate tools that help to overcome some of their limitations, especially as they might relate to the technical and conceptual barriers we have discussed. These include techniques such as multi-criteria analysis (MCA) and multi-criteria decision making (MCDM), Bayesian methods and a set of methods that collectively might be referred to as 'Fuzzy GIS'.

Multi-criteria methods

The overall goal of all such methods is effectively to deal with uncertainty and help an analyst reduce the risks of working with intuition alone. Multi-criteria methods are not unique to spatial analysis, although geographical problems seem to be particularly well suited to them. As their name implies, multi-criteria tools allow various different tests and criteria, based on relevant spatial information, to be simultaneously evaluated to help arrive at some form of 'optimal' answer. They are widely used in location problems, where the goal might be to find the best location given knowledge of requirements and factors that render particular locales suitable, and a sense of the relative weights that should be attached to each. As such, multi-criteria tools exhibit a close fundamental relationship to utility maximisation – that is, to finding the configuration of circumstances that will yield the most benefits while minimising costs. If costs and benefits can be conceptualised clearly and have a logical relationship to geography, then a MCDM framework might be an attractive option for situating an analysis of the overall problem. They are therefore best suited to such problems where a relatively limited number of easily mapped and monetised factors may interact in predictable ways.

The appraisal of different options for a new highway route or wind farm location provides classic examples of the application of multi-criteria methods (notwithstanding that they tend to downplay the importance of political factors, which are clearly also of great importance in such problems). Input factors such as proximity to existing transport networks, elevation, slope, shelter, together with data on historical climatic conditions, can all be easily modelled and integrated within a GIS environment. All that remains is for the analyst to attach some credible weights to each factor (or run various scenarios that test the sensitivity of the solution to different schemes of weights), and produce maps showing varying levels of optimality for the location (see Figure 9.2).

Despite the obvious attraction of using an MCDM approach for many planning problems such as looking for optimal sites for infrastructure, there remains the need to consider how to account for phenomena such as political contestation, community opposition or different subjective assessments of economic value. Left unchecked, the solutions presented by an MCDM analysis will tend to over-emphasise 'technical' or 'mappable' criteria at the cost of more subjective measures. Multi-criteria methods are also less suitable for problems where the relative importance attached to different factors is unknown, or where concepts or phenomena are more 'fuzzy' and less bounded. For example, there may be no robust evidence that can be used to pinpoint the weightings to be attached to 'visual intrusion' in an assessment of wind turbine locations. At the very least, where a degree of uncertainty exists around measurement or weightings, multi-criteria approaches may need to be combined with other techniques such as the use of Bayesian statistics or 'Fuzzy GIS'.

Figure 9.2   *Simplified example of equally weighted multi-criteria analysis (MCA) applied to a wind farm location problem*

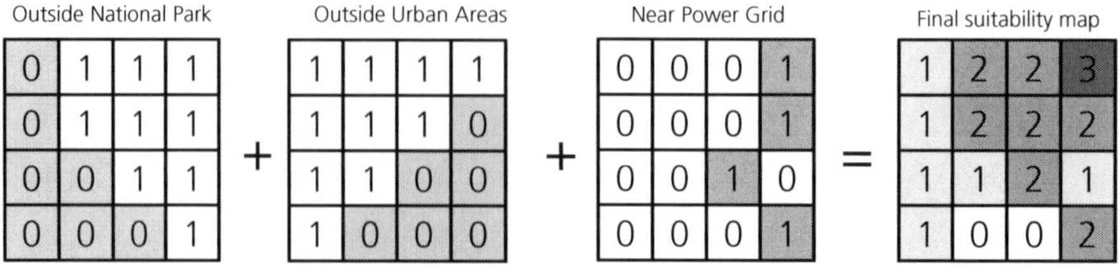

Outside National Park   Outside Urban Areas   Near Power Grid   Final suitability map

Bayesian approaches

While most quantitative analysis techniques rely on the interpretation of probabilities to determine, Bayesian methods seek to incorporate information on prior experiences, beliefs and expert views to help weight a probability distribution. This makes them particularly suited to complex problems, such as in the multi-criteria examples above, where datasets might interact in unknown ways or where there is a lack of empirical data to help guide the analyst in the setting of realistic, credible or data-driven weights. An example would be using remote sensing (satellite) data to classify land use cover. Using known information on the probabilities of different land uses occurring can help the classification procedure – tools in ArcGIS and other GIS packages have been developed that use Bayesian methods to incorporate knowledge from previous experience to improve estimates of statistical analysis routines.

'Fuzzy GIS'

Perhaps disappointingly, 'Fuzzy GIS' is nothing to do with the (alleged) propensity for male GIS users to neglect facial shaving rituals. Instead, it has been developed as a way of overcoming the inappropriately (and improbably) sharp distinctions that GIS otherwise requires – for example, objects being in or out of a zone, or the artificial 'step' in elevation implied by a contour line. Fuzzy GIS can also help in dealing with the uncertainties that are introduced to models by using data collected at the wrong scale (see Chapter 3). Instead of saying something is a member of one class or another, the inputs to a fuzzy tool are a measure of the probability of being in that class (from 0 to 1). So, for example, a traditional tool within GIS for modelling terrain might require a value which is a spot measurement of the angle of the slope. Within raster models, the veracity of a cell value might depend on the context of those around it. Near a ridge where slope changes, there may be far less confidence that the slope representation is precisely right. In a fuzzy model a probability would be attached to the measure – for example, 1 = absolutely certain that the land is flat; 0 = absolutely certain that it is not; 0.5 might mean 50% chance it is flat. So, value can be used to model uncertainty around other sharp boundaries. The attraction of fuzzy logic models within GIS is that they provide a much closer approximation to the way that human beings process information and make decisions. Humans rarely know information definitively, but apply heuristics and sophisticated (unconscious) assessment of probability. They might 'know something when they see it', but not be able to provide a definitive threshold or cut-off value to help with definition. Fuzzy logic models allow membership classes to overlap according to a probability distribution.

In practice, this means that natural language criteria like 'near', 'far', 'within', 'flat' and so on can be operationalised in a more realistic way within a multi-criteria analysis. For each measure, a probability distribution can be applied which is taken into account within the analysis. Figure 9.3 provides a simple example of how this might work in the example of an analysis of site suitability

Figure 9.3   *Example of fuzzy membership distributions for 'steep' and 'noisy', with final suitability map*

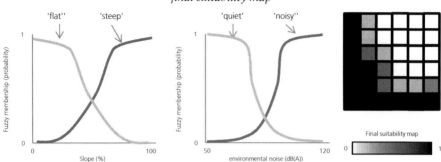

given two criteria: that the site should not be too steep and should not be too noisy. Rather than classify every grid square as either 'quiet' or 'noisy', or 'flat' or 'steep', the probability of membership of those categories is determined using the measured values plotted against a fuzzy membership distribution. These probabilities can then be combined logically to produce a final suitability map (for example using *map algebra* in ArcGIS or similar functions in other packages).

Maps as dialogue

Throughout this chapter, we have discussed some of the practical limits that can be placed on the role of GIS as a decision-making tool. We also reviewed a number of variants of multi-criteria methods that can be used, with care, to help integrate spatial information into an overall decision-making architecture.

In this chapter's introduction, we noted the 'communicative turn' in planning theory that began in earnest in the late 1990s and the subsequent orientation of spatial planning practice towards more collaborative and inclusionary approaches. Central to these processes are an understanding of power relations, a self-awareness or reflexivity on the part of the planner to understand their own practices and positionality, and a recognition that dialogue and consensus-building activities can generate new forms of understanding in opposition to conventional, 'techno-rational' knowledge. Yet, rather than diminish the role of GIS, we feel that seeing planning as a communicative art form in fact emphasises the potential importance of spatial forms of knowledge that are authentic, open to challenge, and sensitive to the diverse ways that knowledge is socially constructed and that planning problems as well as their possible resolutions are conceptualised.

We best understand maps as a system of communication, like speech, text, photos and any other media. They are symbolic abstractions of reality that rely on visual conventions to convey meaning, and, as such, they are malleable through conscious and unconscious decisions on the part of the cartographer.

Moreover, in the case of conveying the results or implications of spatial analysis, the meaning and power inscribed within a map result not only from its cartographic composition, but also fundamentally from the data and methods that underpin them. Like most systems of human communication, maps are a sophisticated and infinitely flexible tool.

What benefits might maps bring to an overall project of communicative policy making or decision making? First, maps can democratise access to 'spatial' understandings of complex problems or phenomena that can complement other forms of knowledge. Spatial context may render visible aspects of a problem that were previously hidden from view. Maps can provide a synopsis, at a range of scales, of the basic issues underpinning a particular decision. But, as is well known, maps can also be abused, and the responsibilities of the analyst and cartographer are great. As Monmonier (1996) noted,

> Like the author of any scholarly work or artistic creation based on reality, the conscientious map author not only examines a variety of sources but relies on extensive experience with the information or region portrayed.
>
> (p. 42)

This gives rise to the second potential benefit. Just as misuse of maps can represent a gross abuse of power, it is equally the case that they can help to overcome or reduce the asymmetric or unequal access to information that may be enjoyed by different communities. When decisions are denuded of their spatial context, distorted constructions of reality may be used to dominate debate. Maybe democratising access to spatial data and the ability to map it can help to counter 'fake news'! If a map or output from a spatial analysis can be used to oppress, they can just as easily speak truth to power. Traditionally, the realm of the analyst and cartographer was that of the expert, and the tools they used (especially in the form of data) were tightly controlled and rationed economically. The past few decades bear witness to incredible progress in opening up access to spatial information. Maps can help rebalance informational power by affording less-advantaged communities or participants in a debate the same access to situational awareness as experts or vested interests.

Third, maps provide the possibility of generating more intuitive presentations of complex issues, mostly in addition to or alongside other types of information. The presentation of quantitative data using a map may be particularly well suited to those for whom spreadsheets induce fear. Patterns of variation may be grasped more intuitively when subject to an appropriate cartographic visualisation.

In each case, it is incumbent on the analyst, the commissioner of the analysis and the cartographer alike to understand their privileged role in shaping information into knowledge, and that their decisions and actions are never neutral or value-free. Critically, there is a need to understand the ethics of using maps in a balanced, fair, proportionate way, without deliberately intending to deceive. Ethical oversight of research within academic communities is now well established within universities and R&D centres, but is arguably less well attuned to the ethical issues bound up in spatial analysis specifically. Local government planners and developers, as well as the consultants they may both employ, are rarely bound by ethical codes pertaining to their work as de facto research. The ethics of information and power are – or should be – important elements of GIS training. Spatial analysis and cartography issues should be integrated with general 'planning ethics' courses and similar.

Bringing it all together – our key points

This book is intended as a practical volume. We did not want it to be a step-by-step guide. Yet we were also keen that it was not too theoretical or abstract. We wanted those working in fields like planning or the built environment professions to see clearly how GIS could be made to work for them, either directly or through the agency of others. This was about how GIS could be effectively and fairly applied in the pursuit of a wider endeavour. How such an endeavour is articulated and rationalised is to some extent in the reader's gift – it seems to us that the art and science of planning for the betterment of the built environment and to pursue goals of economic, social or environmental equity are laudable enough aims.

Maps have been under attack as the pendulum has swung so far away from the 'rational' planning systems of the post-war years. And rightly so. It is right and proper for those involved in the generation, collection, use, analysis and presentation of spatial information to be subject to a critical gaze, for they occupy a position of privilege and power. Oversight makes the technology better and its use more likely to bring about long-lasting benefits for society.

In Chapter 1, we tried to dismantle the reverence sometimes held for GIS users. We place GIS and the use of maps squarely at the heart of the planning and allied professions, not tangential to them. We conceptualise planning as a communicative art, and with it the idea that maps are tools to be deployed alongside other tools in the furtherance of a wider planning project in society which is about mediation of conflict rather than the righteous path.

We developed these themes in Chapter 2. We described the role of GIS in describing our world. We are unashamed when we extol the virtues of description, as part of a journey towards understanding. To know how to analyse something demands that we first are able to describe it. We also acknowledge that there is now an identifiable discipline around GIS. There are professionals that harbour enormous intellectual resources in the development and application of scientific spatial methods. These methods, and their practitioners, are of enormous value – but, as we show throughout the book, they must not sit alone, nor should we reify them. It was also in Chapter 2, therefore, that we first developed a core theme around GIS as a platform for engagement and communication.

In Chapter 3, we turned the traditional view of GIS on its head by focusing on its credentials as a 'spatially enabled' database of our world, rather than primarily a cartographic tool. This served to focus attention on the lifeblood of spatial analysis and map-making: data. We introduced the concepts of structured data and offered a brief introduction to the database architecture that underpins how GIS software works. By thinking about GIS in this way, we hope that the wider analytical possibilities of GIS and spatial analysis might become apparent – the possibilities of new geographical insights that arise through data combination, linkage and formal relationships, rather than simply via spatial coincidence or overlay. We spent some time discussing 'spatial ontologies' – or ways of representation. Whether driven by data science or cartographic principles, GIS is an abstraction, a model, a system of representation and its successful use demands an appreciation of how real-world social or physical phenomena are represented within finite representational systems. The process of linking – or 'joining' – two or more datasets together by virtue of common attributes or common geography is perhaps the key fundamental skill we would wish students and practitioners to acquire.

Chapter 4 was about data. We described it above as 'lifeblood' – it is also the 'currency' that is traded between communities. And why? In the pursuit, we argue, of wisdom. In Chapter 4, we map out an epistemic journey from data through information, knowledge and ultimately to wisdom (DIKW). The key limitations and pitfalls of using data were explored, and we discussed the 'good', the 'bad' and the 'ugly' associated particularly with the enormous rise of openly available and accessible spatial datasets across the globe.

In Chapter 5, we returned again to the theme of communication. We explore the vast potential of GIS as a visualisation tool, by drawing on lessons from visual and communicative science. We implore analysts and planners not to dismiss the importance of visualising data as an essential and integral step in any process of understanding. For all the dizzying possibilities within contemporary GIS software – paid for and free – we extol the virtues of simplicity.

Chapter 6 reviews some of the key techniques for the production of effective and, hopefully, not misleading maps and spatial analyses. We looked at techniques for classifying data, symbolisation, scale, generalisation and flow mapping, and we reviewed (hopefully too evangelically) the components of a 'good' map.

Chapters 7 and 8 introduced some more advanced spatial analysis concepts and techniques. We tried to embed these within real-life practical examples. The 'First Law of Geography' was discussed, and its central role in defining and enabling spatial analysis. We define 'space' and discuss the centrality of spatial concepts in a range of historical and contemporary planning problems. We look at the power of simple techniques like buffering, and the potential of more advanced concepts like network analysis. We discuss the limits of Euclidean approaches to distance, and the exciting potential for planners of network analysis which aims to more closely model 'real-life' costs gradients associated with differential accessibility.

Finally, in this chapter we have offered a cautiously optimistic view of the possibilities of GIS in helping to inform better decisions, policies and plans by encouraging those involved in using GIS or its outputs to engage critically with its role and limitations. We urge caution in adopting a gung-ho attitude to deploying GIS to solve any problem, in any context, and instead counsel for a clear understanding of the organisational, conceptual and technical impediments to successful adoption. We review the role of multi-criteria decision support methods and several associated techniques and tools for helping to 'soften the edges' of spatial constructs as they exist within GIS analyses. We also briefly discuss GIS from an ethical standpoint.

Concluding remarks

GIS offers huge potential. It has driven, and lies behind, some of the biggest corporate advances in the use of data and data science in recent decades, and we live in a truly spatially aware world. For planners and those involved in the management, protection and development of the build environment, that potential has barely been scratched. There is a lot more we could do to let GIS live up to its promise.

GIS should be harnessed for good. It helps us understand, and its democratisation helps reduce information and power asymmetries. Viewed through this lens, GIS is less about colonising power and claiming epistemic territory, and more a tool for communication.

GIS lets us see. It opens up a world of visualisation that spreadsheet models can never hope to rival. It helps us make links between phenomena on the basis of the attribute that is common to so much of what goes on in our world – the attribute of *where*.

It is hoped that this book has provided an exciting insight into the ways that GIS and spatial analysis, and the increasingly open resources that underpin them, can be used not just by experts and consultants, but by communities, individuals and multi-disciplinary teams with a stake in the planning of our built environments.

References

Boulding, K. (1970) *Economics as a Science*, New York: McGraw-Hill.

Brewer, C. A. (2005) *Designing Better Maps: A Guide for GIS Users*, 1st edn, Redlands, CA: ESRI Press.

Campbell, H. and Marshall, R. (2002) Utilitarianism's bad breath? A re-evaluation of the public interest justification for planning. *Planning Theory*, 1(2), 163–87.

Campbell, S. (1996) Green cities, growing cities, just cities?: Urban planning and the contradictions of sustainable development. *Journal of the American Planning Association*, 62(3), 296–312.

Cook W. J. (2014) *In Pursuit of the Traveling Salesman: Mathematics at the Limits of Computation*, Princeton: Princeton University Press.

Dahlgren, A. (2008) *Geographic Accessibility Analysis: Methods and Application Real Estate Science*, Lund: Department of Technology and Society, Lund University.

de Smith, M., Goodchild, M. and Longley, P. (2018) *Geospatial Analysis: A Comprehensive Guide to Principles Techniques and Software Tools*, 6th edn. Troubador Publishing, Leicester.

Dijkstra, E. W. (1959) *A note on two problems in connexion with graphs. Numerische Mathematik*, 1, 269–71.

Dorling, D. (1991) The visualization of spatial structure (PhD Thesis, Department of Geography, University of Newcastle upon Tyne).

Douglas, D. and Peucker, T. (1973) Algorithms for the reduction of the number of points required to represent a digitized line or its caricature. *The Canadian Cartographer*, 10(2), 112–22.

Duckham, M., Goodchild, M. F. and Worboys, M. F. (eds.) (2003) *Foundations of Geographic Information Science*, London: Taylor & Francis.

ESRI (1998) *ESRI Shapefile Technical Description: An ESRI White Paper – July 1998*, Redlands, CA: ESRI.

ESRI (2015) *Dasymetric Mapping* [Entry in ESRI GIS Dictionary]. Available at: https://support.esri.com/en/other-resources/gis-dictionary/term/3ccc2efa-e7c7-4b11-9903-2c00895bc74a.

ESRI (2018) *GIS Dictionary: GIScience*. Available at: https://support.esri.com/en/other-resources/gis-dictionary/term/9f04737b-f242-4131-93b1-921bbbae40b9.

ESRI (n.d.) Algorithms used by the ArcGIS Network Analyst extension (website). Available at http://desktop.arcgis.com/en/arcmap/latest/extensions/network-analyst/algorithms-used-by-network-analyst.htm.

Ferrari, E. and Green, M. (2013) Travel to school and housing markets: A case study of Sheffield, England. *Environment and Planning A*, 45(11), 2771–88.

Field, K. (2018) *Cartography*, Redlands, CA: ESRI Press.

Heathcote, P. M. (2003) *A-Level ICT*, 3rd edn, Ipswich: Payne-Gallway.

Huff, D. (1954) *How to Lie with Statistics*, Norton, New York.

Kent, R. B. and Klosterman, R. E. (2000) GIS and mapping: Pitfalls for planners. *Journal of the American Planning Association*, 66(2), 189–98.

Kirtland Wright, J. (1938) *Notes on Statistical Mapping: With Special Reference to the Mapping of Population Phenomena*, Washington, DC: American Geographical Society and Population Association of America.

Klosterman, R. (1985) Arguments for and against planning. *The Town Planning Review*, 56(1), 5–20.

Lake, R. W. (1993) Planning and applied geography: Positivism, ethics, and geographic information systems. *Progress in Human Geography*, 17(3), 404–13.

Lazer, D., Kennedy, R., King, G., and Vespignani, A. (2014) The parable of Google Flu: Traps in big data analysis. *Science*, 343(6176), 1203–05.

Longley, P., Goodchild, M., Maguire, D. and Rhind, D. (2015) *Geographic Information Systems and Science*, 4th edn, London: Wiley.

Monmonier, M. (1996) *How to Lie with Maps*, 2nd rev. edn, Chicago: University of Chicago Press.

Nelson G. D. and Rae, A. (2016) An economic geography of the United States: From commutes to megaregion's. *PLoSONE*, 11(11), 1–23.

Obermeyer, N. J. and Pinto, J. K. (2007) *Managing Geographic Information Systems*, 2nd edn, New York: Guildford Press.

Openshaw, S. (1983) *The Modifiable Areal Unit Problem*, Norwich: Geo Books.

Open Knowledge International (2019) *What Is Open Data*. Available at: http://opendatahandbook.org/guide/en/what-is-open-data/

Peterson, G. (2009) *GIS Cartography: A Guide to Effective Map Design*, Boca Raton, FL: CRC Press.

Pickles, J. (ed.) (1995) *Ground Truth. The Social Implications of Geographic Information Systems*, New York: Guilford Press.

Playfair, W. (1801) *The Statistical Breviary*, London.

Rae, A. (2009) From spatial interaction data to spatial interaction information? Geovisualisation and spatial structures of migration from the 2001 UK census. *Computers, Environment and Urban Systems*, 33, 161–78.

Rae, A. (2014) Featured graphic. The geography of mortgage lending in London. *Environment and Planning A*, 46(8), 1778–80.

Schrahe, C. (2015) *Die Liste der 100 größten Skigebiete der Welt*, Cologne: Montenius Consult.

Scottish Government (2014) *Scottish Government Urban Rural Classification 2013–2014*, Edinburgh: Scottish Government.

Singleton, A. D., Longley, P. A., Allen, R. and O'Brien, O. (2011) Estimating secondary school catchment areas and the spatial equity of access. *Computers, Environment and Urban Systems*, 35(3), 241–49.

Storper, M. and Scott, A. J. (2016) Current debates in urban theory: A critical assessment. *Urban Studies*, 53, 1114–36.

Sui, D. (2004) Tobler's First Law of Geography: A big idea for a small world?. *Annals of the Association of American Geographers*, 94(2), 269–77.

Tobler, W. (1970) A computer movie simulating urban growth in the Detroit region. *Economic Geography*, 46(2), 234–40.

Tobler, W. (1987) Experiments in migration mapping by computer. *The American Cartographer*, 14(2), 155–63.

Tobler, W. (2000) Movement talk. Available at: http://www.geog.ucsb.edu/~tobler/presentations/Movement-talk.pdf.

Tobler, W. (2004) 'On the First Law of Geography: A Reply', *Annals of the Association of American Geographers*, 94(2), 304-310.

Tomlinson, R. F. (1967) *An Introduction to the Geographic Information System of the Canada Land Inventory*, Ottawa: Department of Forestry and Rural Development.

Uitermark, J. and Boy, J. D. (2017) Reassembling the city through Instagram. *Transactions of the Institute of British Geographers*, 42(4), 612–24.

Wolfe, P. J., Yim, S. H., Lee, G., Ashok, A., Barrett, S. R. H. and Waitz, I. A. (2014) Near-airport distribution of the environmental costs of aviation. *Transport Policy*, 34, 102–08.

Index

Please note: page numbers in **bold type** indicate figures or illustrations, those in *italics* indicate tables or breakout boxes.